Quit Taking Your Own Bad Advice

How to Stop Overthinking and Start Following the Brilliance of Others

DR. TERRY WAGER AND
CHRISTINE MCGINLEY

Quit Taking Your Own Bad Advice: How to Stop Overthinking and Start Following the
Brilliance of Others
Copyright © 2020 by Dr. Terry Wager and Christine McGinley

Manufactured in the United States of America.

ISBN: 978-1-953586-20-9

ACKNOWLEDGEMENTS

In the spirit our following the brilliance of others, we would like to thank a few key people we have crossed paths with on our journey of writing this book. Generator Coaching would be nothing without all the people who have believed in us helped us along the way and we are forever grateful.

To Karen, Claudia and all the awesome folks at Hybrid Global Publishing. You have been incredibly helpful in the process and walked me through all of my questions as a new author.

To my mom and dad who believed in me even when I didn't believe in myself. Through your support and firm, but fair, love I was able to make it through my struggles and came out stronger for it. Thank you so much for all you did in my life. I will always love you both so very much.

To all of my professors, supervisors and psychology mentors who helped my shape my point of view. Without your wisdom and knowledge and rigor I would be one hell of a Chef.

To my numerous clients throughout my years of work, I appreciate all of you who suggested I write this book. I have been so fortunate to have so many amazing clients who trusted me to help them grow and change. I am honored to have been with each of you on your personal journeys of growth and transformation.

To all of our previous coaches and mentors, you have inspired Christine and me. You believed in us along our journey. Your faith in us meant the world to us as we trudge these new roads.

A special thanks to Larry Winget. Thank for your guidance and direction on this project. This project was not even on our radar last year at this time. Christine and I truly appreciate your wisdom and feedback and great sense of humor as you directed us to be clear on our point of view and take a stand for what we believe.

A very special thanks to our coach Suzanne Evans, and mentors Amanda Evans and Susan Brady with your belief, straight up advice, direction and encouragement we took our business to new levels previously only dreamed of. We are so grateful for you and the whole Driven team. We feel blessed to have you in our lives.

Finally to my partner in business and life, Christine, I could not be luckier and more blessed that to have you in my life. You make every day exciting, fun and worth every minute. I could not think of a better partner or friend. I am so grateful for all your help bringing structure to my abstract ideas that help create real lasting transformation for all those we help.

READY FOR THE BULLET TRAIN?

Job stress costs US industry over 300 billion in annually in health costs, absenteeism, and poor work performance. We know that Emotional Mastery is the solution. If all of your overthinking has you stuck, hurting your performance or causing you to hate what you do, this is the time to master your emotions. Our simple Emotional Mastery Process is easy to implement with Dr. Terry Wager's concrete coaching and training. This is where transformation happens so you can truly generate the business, relationships and life you desire. www.emotionalmastery.com

TABLE OF CONTENTS

Introduction: Why Is Self-Improvement So Hard? 1

Chapter 1: The Lie Machine 7

Chapter 2: The Noise in the World 15

Chapter 3: Your Brain's Broken Filtration System 29

Chapter 4: Fixing the Filter 39

Chapter 5: Learning to Trust Yourself 51

Chapter 6: Trusting in the Brilliance of Others 61

Chapter 7: Committing to Action 71

Chapter 8: Making a Decision 81

Chapter 9: Accelerating Your Growth 89

INTRODUCTION

Why Is Self-Improvement So Hard?

We all want success in our lives. We want more money to pay our bills and to retire with comfort. We want great health and fulfilling relationships. We want to feel as if our work is aligned with our own values and priorities. So why is it that so many of us live paycheck to paycheck? Why don't we have financial security, physical fitness, or a sense of purpose?

The simple fact is we tend to sabotage our own success by listening to ourselves and doing what we think is best instead of asking for help from qualified people. We keep taking our own bad advice and then wonder why it doesn't work out.

Breaking that cycle is what this book is all about. In the coming pages, I will share with you how to identify and tune out the unhelpful voices—the chitter-chatter in your own mind. Then, I am going to share a way you can start truly trusting in your own brilliance as well as relying on the brilliance of experts. Along the way you'll learn how to achieve the goals you set, pursue your dreams, and find that next level of success you've been working so hard for.

At this point you might be asking: "How do I know this will work for me?" That's an incredibly common question, and a perfect example of why you need to keep reading. This question is a strong indicator of someone who truly wants an answer. It is also a sign that the person asking that question has had unfulfilled promises before. It is a sign of a person who has become skeptical—a person who has started falling into the habit of judging before they fully understand. If this is you, what does it say that you are only a few paragraphs into a new book and your own mind is making you skeptical of advice that has worked for thousands of other people?

Well, you are not alone. As a society, we've been taught to trust ourselves over everyone else. We carry around an inherent belief that we will make good decisions, especially if we take our time to really consider all the angles and possibilities. That's why we labor over them, thinking about them endlessly until they paralyze us. We may even occasionally discuss them with others, though we almost always ultimately decide to follow our own course of action instead of acting on expert advice. We make the same choices again and again—based on the same faulty ideas and assumptions— keeping us stuck in a pattern of thoughts and actions that leave us unfulfilled.

Let's face it: most of us aren't making the money we want to make. We are not living the life we desire because we are getting in our own way. We do this by relying on our own bad information. As a result, we keep coming up short. That causes frustration and anxiety, which push us to try even harder to make things happen in our career or business. However, the majority of people just implement a more intense version of the same old strategy they were already not getting results with. It seems that no matter how much they work hard and attempt to grow, they never quite get ahead.

Many of us feel like we're busier than ever trying to grow our business and increase our profits. We are striving to create something amazing and sustainable—not just a business that generates wealth, but a legacy that can evolve over time. And yet it seems as if all we actually create is a vicious cycle of obstacles, busy work, and stress about unnecessary tasks that never truly move us to our vision.

This experience can be incredibly frustrating, and unfortunately it is the rule rather than the exception. Too many of us have been paying attention and working hard to reach the finish line only to realize that our attention was on the wrong things. Even worse, we were listening to the wrong information all along. The reality is, we're all so busy overthinking, second-guessing, and hesitating about what's next that momentum fades. Doubt creeps in, and we can't take the actions that will generate the results we truly want. We become completely caught up in making plans, but then never execute them. We are so busy agonizing over how to get everything done that we totally miss the bigger picture.

Does this sound like you? Are you operating from a place of hope, wishing your plans would work? If so, how does it benefit you to jump from one ineffective plan to the next if all that movement comes to nothing? This downward spiral brings more stress than income, wearing you down day by day. Many of you might even feel burned out by everything that's been happening—if so, you've made the right choice to pick up this book.

I've seen this cycle many times with my clients, and it's a sign that they are acting out an unconscious pattern that would never generate results. Contrary to what common mindset training is attempting to sell us, we can't think our way into new actions. We've got to act our way into new thinking.

Business leaders and gurus often stress the importance of working smart over working hard. Taking your own bad advice is the ultimate example of getting that idea the wrong way around. It doesn't matter how many hours you put in, how many phone calls you make, or how many items you cross off your "to-do" list. As C.S. Lewis says, "Progress is not worth much if we are progressing down the wrong road."

We still fail—just with the extra pain of having broken our backs to get to rock bottom. If my words come across like a breath of fresh air, that's good. If you can relate to what I'm saying and it seems like I'm talking to you, that's even better. As you will come to understand in a new way, all behavioral change comes from emotional shifts.

In order for you to hear and act on this message, I need you to get a little bit angry. If you find yourself questioning or feeling a little defensive, investigate that. Notice that. Experience that as the beginning of an awakening. I've been through this process myself, and I know exactly what it's like to have your mind opened in a new way.

My experiences as a psychologist, coach, and human being living on planet Earth have taught me that most people don't want to take action outside of their comfort zone until circumstances force them to. People who do take action have to be challenged in ways that trigger them to question their attitudes and assumptions. I'm not going to sugarcoat things. because that's not what anyone needs. Political correctness and pulling punches have never helped anyone grow, and I wouldn't be doing my job. My role is to get the people I help to face up to reality and truly take different actions that get results.

As you might have noticed already, this isn't like other professional development books. I'm not going to tell you to find your big "why" or tell you the answer is to achieve the perfect work-life balance. I won't snow you by simply encouraging you to work on maintaining a positive mindset in the midst of your current circumstances. I definitely won't suggest that manifestation will provide you with the life you want or pretend that you can just create a good habit in as little as twenty-one days that will take you to success. Instead, I'm going to disrupt your unconscious patterns and show you a fresh approach for generating the results and life you desire.

Creating the change you want requires you to have a new approach to thinking, but it doesn't mean overthinking. And really, that might be the biggest challenge in front of you: to consider and accept ideas without dwelling on them. It will also require you to have an open mind and really look deep inside yourself because that is where all our most transformational experiences start. Deep down inside every man, woman, and child is a fundamental desire for growth that becomes obscured by the noise of the world.

Many in my position say, "You're going to have to trust me." I disagree. I don't want you to trust me. I don't want you to take my word for it. Read this book with a willingness to explore what I have to offer. See what might be true and helpful. It will help if you simply decide *right now* that you're going to give it a shot and follow through without questioning too much of what will happen later. As I'll explain further in the book, this approach is one sure way I know to get the results you want.

To date, I've already helped thousands of people make miraculous transformations in their lives and careers. Of course, my process will never be perfect, and neither will I. I still come up short on my own goals from time to time and get distracted by the noise of the world. My program is constantly evolving, as it has been since I first began my educational and professional journey. While I might not have every detail or answer etched in stone, I can tell you that I *do* have a foundational platform that fills the holes that exist in many other coaching systems. Most people who have come to me already have learned so many different techniques and strategies, adding program after program in hopes of finding that one thing that is going to create their success. My proven strategy weaves all the other techniques and strategies together to generate a solid plan for exploding your growth. You can finally start taking the right action to achieve your goals you and generate the money and life you desire.

If you are someone who is already making a multiple six- or seven-figure income, this book might not be for you. If you're too stubborn, prideful, or afraid to accept guidance, then you can save us both a lot of time and put it down now. However, if you're someone in the world of business who feels frustrated and unfocused, I can help. Better yet, if you are doing great and want to make even more money, free up more time and energy for new adventures, and learn to trust in your own brilliance and rely on the brilliance of others, then you have found the resource you've been looking for.

In the coming chapters, I'm going to share with you why traditional self-improvement plans fail. I'll share my perspective on how we get "stuck," go over all the filters that keep us trapped in mediocrity, and explain why it's so important to implement advice and direction from qualified people who have our growth in mind. I'll cover how to find voices you can trust, as well as how to spot those with questionable suggestions or motivations. And finally, I'll provide a clear, proven strategy to take action, while removing stress and exploding your income.

Are you ready to quit taking your own bad advice? Let's jump in!

CHAPTER 1

The Lie Machine

Most of the people I meet can immediately relate to the idea that the noise of life is drowning out their goals and dreams. What is harder to accept is the notion that the distorted sounds and echoes are coming almost exclusively from their own minds.

It would be great to blame this phenomenon on the media, technology, or some other bogeyman. Unfortunately, this book is about facts. And the indisputable fact is this: the lies you believe—the ones that stop you from being focused, productive, and an emotionally balanced high performer—come from the falsehood factory that sits between your ears.

From tiny white lies to giant-sized whoppers, your mind generates an endless stream of ideas that simply don't have much basis in reality. It actually has a good reason for doing this (more on that in a second), but it's nearly impossible to move yourself forward without facing up to this truth. Ignore it and you'll be stuck in a cycle of what ifs that hamper your ability to make plans. And you'll be tempted to blame everyone and everything else for what goes wrong. However, other people aren't the problem, and neither are circumstances. It's all about the lies we tell ourselves.

Why We Lie to Ourselves Again and Again

We have all heard it before. Each of us is our own worst enemy. We almost have to be; evolution has conspired to make us that way.

Consider this. At one point in our history there were physical threats lurking all over the place. We couldn't ignore them, not even once, if we wanted to survive and pass on our genes. And so, a little bit of paranoia was a healthy thing. Our primitive brain had to develop in such a way that it could pick out potential threats very rapidly and clearly. Otherwise we would fall down a hole or get eaten pretty quickly.

To see this phenomenon in action, imagine the way you feel when you see a scary movie. Consciously, you know you're sitting in a safe theater. You have your popcorn and drink in your lap. You *paid* to be there, after all. When someone jumps out of a dark corner on-screen, though, it's very natural to react. In that split second your mind is reacting to a potential threat. In this situation the fright is fun and exciting. However, your mind does this because it can't afford to take an hour and a half off. It needs to deal with each potential crisis as a serious one-off event. If it didn't, something might slip through and get you while you were caught unaware.

Now, you might be thinking to yourself that you don't watch scary movies and you are not in danger of being eaten by a predator. Maybe not, but we all encounter thousands of real and—more importantly—imagined threats to our safety, self-image, and sense of ego every day. Therein lies the problem. Our protective filter reacts to imagined threats just as if they are real.

Our brain, doing the one thing it's best at, is always reacting to our unconscious emotional experience. It's in the background constantly analyzing what might happen to us in any given situation, or with a certain set of circumstances. It continually asks the dreaded "what ifs," pelting us again and again with what might happen. Even worse, because the perceived threats come so quickly, it abbreviates the process and treats imaginary crises as if they were already occurring. This, in turn, triggers even more emotion that we again react to. Are you starting to understand how this could make someone feel scared or even defensive a majority of the time?

I like to describe self-talk like one of those old-time ticker tapes investors used to follow. All day long the ticker tape machine would spit out transactions, prices, and details so an interested person could get a sense of what was happening in the market. These ticker tapes were useful, but they didn't really provide any reason or reassurance for fluctuations. In the case of a stock market crash, they would reinforce the sense of impending doom more and more strongly with each passing minute.

In 1929, so much bad news spilled out of ticker tapes across Manhattan that scared and despairing stockbrokers threw themselves from skyscrapers. They weren't being chased by wolves or thrown to their deaths. They simply jumped because they believed the lie machine. Their heads told them they were broke and would never recover. It told them they were going to lose their jobs, and that their homes would be taken and their wives would leave. The news coming out of their minds was that they'd never be able to feed their children, that the world had come to an end, and their life was over. Might as well jump.

Back in reality, the news was bad, but it wasn't *that* bad. Their lie machines were running at full tilt. The noise in their heads was so overpowering they could not think things through rationally.

Today we have CNN, FOX News, as well as social media or even old memories feeding us lies. Wherever the lies come from, they add up quickly. When our minds are feeding us one terrible thought after another, for even the strongest of us high performers, it can cause hurdles. For many others struggling to increase performance, it can be almost insurmountable to find the strength to persevere and some days to even get out of bed. Working a plan of personal or career development may be virtually impossible under those circumstances. The terrible and defeating thoughts are difficult to let go of, however, simply because we become so attached to them.

Sometimes the Lie Is More Comfortable Than the Truth

The lies we tell ourselves amount to a security blanket that keeps us safely wrapped up in our own circumstances. That makes them tough to let go of, even in situations where our conscious minds wish we could let go of the supposed comfort and get a taste of freedom.

Or to put it another way, we tend to stick to our own stories and delusions even when they don't really make sense. One of my mentors used to joke, "This is my story and I'm sticking to it," pointing out that we all tend to believe ourselves over solid evidence.

I have witnessed this again and again, most notably when I was working at the state prison. There was an inmate who was extremely psychotic. He was convinced he was Thor. The well-meaning guards would try to convince this inmate that he was not a mythical godlike superhero and that he had to follow their directions. Every time the guards tried to bring this inmate back to reality, he would become even more agitated. He would start yelling about how he needed to go to his homeland of Valhalla and begin punching himself in the face. Needless to say, that wasn't very productive.

The harder you try to convince someone of reality, the deeper they dig themselves into the story that's playing out in their minds. By trying to change Thor's opinions of reality, the guards established themselves as part of his problem. He began to wonder whether they were involved in conspiracies against him. It created a no-win situation. This guy was psychotic, but we all do the same thing when our own beliefs about ourselves are challenged. It's human nature.

If that example seems a little extreme, take the case of an otherwise normal, amazingly talented young man who came to me a few years ago because he couldn't shake the feeling he was being affected by some undetectable illness. He had seen doctors, talked with friends, and done his share of online searching. He understood why everyone else thought the problem was in his mind. Still, no matter how much evidence he uncovered suggesting that he was okay, it only convinced him that the illness was undetectable, as he had suspected, and others didn't understand the gravity of his situation.

This otherwise reasonable and educated young man took in the same facts as everyone else—including all the experts—and came to a completely different conclusion than they did. His emotional filter colored the thoughts going through his mind to the point that it was impossible for him to consider viewpoints that didn't match the one he was looking for.

The reality is that we don't make decisions based on facts or reason. We unconsciously see the world through our protective emotional filter or (protective filter from here on out). What we feel is true to us at any given time. If we are not aware of the role our unconscious protective filter plays, then trying to think differently isn't going to work. The same patterns and the same actions will keep coming up again and again.

By the way, I was able to break that pattern for this young man by getting him to ask himself an important question. I'm going to share that question with you in chapter six.

The more we feel vulnerable and exposed to the world, the faster the ticker tape in our mind flows and the more anxiety we create. It accelerates to the point that we see nothing but bad news, even if that isn't what's actually happening in the outside world. Then we get into a state where we are so worried that we lose control and search, sometimes frantically, for coping strategies to make us feel better. Coping strategies or coping mechanisms don't actually improve our situations, but they do allow us hold on to the lies we are so attached to while helping us avoid our vulnerable raw emotions or (raw emotions from here on out). And until we understand this phenomenon, our head will continue creating distractions because that's role of our protective filter—to avoid raw emotions at all cost.

What You Feel Is What You See

Even if you've never taken a Rorschach personality test you are probably familiar with the idea. It's the one where psychologists show inkblots to patients and ask them what they see.

Although these tools are often the basis for humor in pop culture or some dramatic scene in a movie, the fact is that they have a wonderful track record of predicting certain types of behaviors. That's because any interpretation a person gives to an image will be at least somewhat indicative of their worldview or attitude. Even a joke, or an obvious attempt to deflect, will tell you an amazing amount about their filter.

I mention these tests here because they beautifully illustrate the power of emotion as a filter. The way we feel dictates what we think and what we see. This process takes place outside of our own awareness. Because we don't directly notice the filtering taking place, it's very difficult to control or change. There are several "emotional Intelligence" tests available that assess our self-awareness and emotional ability; however, it is easy to skew results. What those tests are looking for is so apparent that their validity is questionable at best. We have to study the effects and then reverse engineer a solution in order to stop taking our own bad advice. This is exactly what you'll learn in this book.

Imagine for a moment that you were exhausted and in a room that had a mattress and a very bright light. You might try covering your eyes up with a blanket or a pillow if you really wanted to get some sleep. Those could work as temporary solutions, but they wouldn't allow you to rest very peacefully. The light would always get back in, and the harder you'd try to block it out, the less comfortable you would be.

That's a good analogy for the situation most of us find ourselves in. The lights in our case are our disturbed emotions that aren't being identified. Instead of "turning them off" and getting back into our balanced, intentional emotional filter, we attempt to "cover them up." We attempt shut them out, or we attempt to distract ourselves so we don't notice them. These distractions can include drinking, drugs, work, shopping, or even wasting time with busy work. We have tons of behaviors to distract ourselves. We tell ourselves we will be happy when we find the perfect job, the perfect partner, or the ultimate vacation. We talk about the need for more. We think we need more money, more time, more sleep, more clarity, and more hours to get away. All the while, we are suffering because we simply haven't addressed the emotions that are causing our lie machine, strapped to our shoulders, to go into high gear telling us having all those things will make us better.

You've noticed it yourself. The vast majority of people are trying to outperform, outthink, and outmaneuver everyone and everything to eke out a miserable existence in this overwhelming universe. Is that how you want to live?

Fulfillment and success don't come from an endless string of experiences or distractions. They can only be found when you're ready to do the hard work of identifying unaddressed emotions. That might sound like a bunch of crap, but it's just basic biology. Until we identify our emotions, our thoughts can't be clear or focused. When our head isn't right, we don't follow through or perform at a high level.

It's a natural human tendency to think, overthink, and worry. Our brains are constructed in such a way that makes us look for risks everywhere. We struggle to make plans because we try to mentally cross bridges before we ever get to them. Then, when we can't work out all the possible outcomes associated with a specific scenario, we end up feeling overwhelmed and give up. But that isn't the end of the story.

All of the tendencies I've described in this chapter are normal and instinctual, but that doesn't make them inevitable. In other words, you can break the cycle if you want to. For that to happen, you have to take a look at the emotional filters your thoughts are coming from. It's easier than you think. In the coming chapters I'm going to show you how.

CHAPTER 2

The Noise in the World

Can you hear it?

Nearly all of us would agree there is too much "noise" in our day-to-day lives. We wake up first thing in the morning to our phones. Social media is ever-present from Facebook, Instagram, and LinkedIn to dozens of other distractors. Our email, text and phone messages all alert us to the day's impending disasters even before our morning coffee. Radio, TV, and dozens of streaming videos and podcasts continuously bombard us. In the Information Age, there is plenty of data but very little insight. Most of us can't figure out what we're doing, where we're going, or how to accomplish our goals because our heads seem to be buzzing all the time.

This noise causes a lot of damage. It keeps us up at night. It stresses us out and causes us to indulge or overeat or check out. It sabotages our relationships and stops us from being honest, intimate, and vulnerable. It holds us back from recognizing our talents and achieving our vision. More importantly, it keeps us stuck at choke points in our businesses and careers, not to mention our relationships or our lives in general. At times it even seduces us to binge on all the mindless TV programs when we know we'd be much better off reading books or working on professional certifications or even writing a book.

Have you ever been cooking in the kitchen and turned on the fan over the stove? You notice the fan, of course. It's intrusive and somewhat bothersome while you are cooking. But you don't actually notice how much it bothers you until you turn it off. The moment you turn it off, your body relaxes. You feel a level of tension simply dissipate as you enjoy the new silence in the room. The noise of the world is that same constant noise, causing a level of distraction, second-guessing, and self-doubt. Often, like the stove fan, you don't even realize it until you have some quiet to notice how loud the world has truly become.

Everyone knows the feeling of this bombardment, but few people really slow down to understand the true source of our distraction. That's why we blame the wrong causes. This outside noise can play a definite role. It's very common nowadays to blame technology for being too distracting. Contrary to what you might think, though, the reason we are unclear and unmotivated does *not* have a lot to do with our phone, the internet, or any other form of technology. It has much more to do with our level of discipline. We let those devices distract us. We are so drawn to those web-connected devices that we succumb to the desire to see what's happening. It's our obsession.

The big stumbling block we all have to deal with—the X factor that holds us back again and again—has mostly to do with ourselves. We struggle to focus because we simply won't quit taking our own bad advice.

Most people push back against this idea. We believe that we make better decisions with the right information. We believe that if we try hard enough, we will figure out the best course of action. We are sure that our biggest problem is the outside noise. We are sure the drama of life is what is causing the distraction and bad decisions.

On January 28, 1986, it was eighteen degrees and a beautiful, unusually crisp morning at Kennedy Space Center. Everyone was enthusiastic about the upcoming launch. Seven astronauts, including—for the first time ever—a teacher, were going on a six-day mission to deploy a satellite. It was supposed to be the Challenger's last mission, but no one expected what happened next to be the reason. Or did they?

Seventy-three seconds after launch, the Challenger tragically exploded, killing all seven astronauts. Everyone was surprised and horrified at the events—well, not everyone. Bob Ebeling, one of the engineers, while still horrified, was not surprised by the explosion. In fact, Bob had warned his engineering colleagues at Morton Thiokol against the launch. He pointed out a flaw in the O-ring seals that prevent burning rocket fuel from leaking out of the booster joints.

Allan McDonald, head of engineering, even attempted to get NASA to abort the mission. So being warned about this fatal flaw, how did this tragedy happen? Was it the outside noise? Did they not have enough information? Was it that they could not concentrate enough to hear the engineers?

In almost every situation in which we have difficulty focusing, most of us can point to something outside of us that is vying for our attention. That just proves my point. None of us wants to think we are wrong, or that we cause our own problems. We are much more comfortable with blaming just about anything or anyone except the person staring back at us in the mirror, even though he or she drives every decision we make.

The truth about the Challenger disaster is that the people in charge listened to their own bad advice rather than relying on the brilliance of their experts, and as a result seven innocent people lost their lives.

It may sound harsh of me to suggest that you are the cause of all your problems. However, this is the best news anyone could give you. This is good news because it takes you out of a victim stance and empowers you to make real change in your life and in your business.

In other words, you don't have to change anyone else's mind or get rid of bad habits or spend precious time trying to keep confusion away. You just have to turn your focus toward yourself and understand the process of growth.

What We've Been Taught about Mindset and Personal Growth Is Wrong

Usually, by the time someone makes their way to us, they have explored a lot of other options. They have picked up countless books, attended countless seminars, and tried countless other types of group and private coaching. They might have even given counseling or therapy a shot. After all of that, they come to us because they want to be high performers and something still sits in their way. They are tired of settling. They want better, more advanced answers and solutions than what they have been given. They want a magic bullet that will change everything. They want the perfect answer to find the success they desire.

Most of these people have a lot of existing ideas about personal growth and development. And sadly, most of them are wrong. Many trainings and programs provide a variety of self-improvement techniques. They have very thought-out conditioning drills. They are loaded with fluffy auto-suggestions, affirmations, and feel-good slogans. Many programs have mind-bending challenges. Gurus convince us we have power by having us walk on glass or break arrows with our throat. These antics are elaborate tricks to prove we can achieve the impossible if we just have the right mindset. Several have mechanical practices such as "If you get rid of certain words like *try* and *can't*, you will overcome the challenges those words bring." Some of these techniques are ludicrous, while others do help, what none of them give is a clear path with a lasting solution.

There is a simple reason for this: most people (including coaches, their clients, and the vast majority of those in the helping or therapy professions) just don't understand how to create lasting change. What they *think* happens is that:

1. A person decides to make changes in their life.
2. They set a lofty goal.
3. They reinforce it with all kinds of popular strategies to make the change stick.

These strategies include motivational recordings, vision boards, coping tools, and other feel-good materials and strategies. The belief is that before long, their thinking will improve. They will then start achieving the results they were looking for. They will become more motivated, which will lead to more positive actions, and so on. For a select few this works.

This is the pure mindset model. The essential idea of this flawed model is that mindset is the key. All you have to do is improve your mindset; your thoughts drive your actions. The model suggests that you can think yourself and talk yourself into doing the things you should do. Even more, you can talk yourself into doing those things better than you were doing them before. "With the right mindset, you can become unstoppable." While this last statement is true, the premise is totally wrong. Mindset is a result of emotional state. Mindset alone is like focusing on the train engine while forgetting it runs on a track. We will go much deeper into this later in the book.

Before we get into the big problem with this type of mindset focus model, ask yourself how successful it has been in your life, or the lives of others you know. Are you at the place you want to be? Are you at the top of your career? Has it taken the exact amount of time you thought it would? How much faster could you move?

If you did change a major habit, congratulations! That's awesome, but how much effort did you exert to make that change?

How many men and women can you point to who have used the power of positive thinking to make a great deal of money, lose lots of weight, or successfully start a business? Can you think of dozens who went from the ground up, or is it more often the case that the people who were already doing well with their goals were using these tools to keep themselves moving? You know the answer and so do I.

This pure mindset model doesn't work because it misrepresents the way humans think and act. It's true that we behave based on our thoughts, but it isn't accurate to say that our thoughts are the beginning of the process. The reality is that we "feel" something before we have a thought to begin with. We have a small, almost imperceptible twinge milliseconds before an idea comes to our minds. We talk about those sensations like they are thoughts, *but they aren't.*

In truth, our emotions come first. They trigger our thoughts, and those thoughts drive us to action.

That's a powerful fact. It means that our thinking is a lot more pattern-based and way more difficult to change. It's not impossible, but it's much more difficult. Now, I don't want to scare anyone away. This isn't a book about getting in touch with your inner child. It *is* about creating amazing change, and that means working with a more realistic, more useful model of the mind that works for any situation.

Emotion is a concept that many talk about but can't really tangibly explain. It is the elephant in the room when it comes to personal development. Many people avoid it because they think it denotes something soft or squishy. A lot of coaches and even mental health professionals start out addressing emotions and then fall right back into talking about thinking and behavior.

Emotional intelligence experts all talk about emotions and emotional IQ or EQ, and then they fall right back into focusing on how to manage behavior rather than relieve emotions. How often have you heard someone say they wanted to "separate facts from emotions" to get to the bottom of an issue? The act of separating is a behavior in and of itself. Furthermore, most people don't really know how to distinguish behavior from emotion. The confusion between emotion and behavior causes most of our difficulties in communicating—with ourselves first and then with others.

Unconscious emotions are the power center of the human being. What we consider and interpret facts to be depends very strongly on the emotions we are experiencing. Addressing emotions doesn't mean we're all going to have a good cry or that we're weak or on the edge of a breakdown. It simply means we experience the "emotions" before we think the "thoughts." Emotions fuel every thought and behavior. Actually if you think about it, thinking is a behavior. It's an action. It's something we do. Thinking and overthinking doesn't change that. Thinking really just intensifies our emotions like gas on a fire, for our benefit or to our detriment.

So how do you defuse the emotion if it's not by thinking, you ask? Well, instead of going into deep thought or analysis about it or searching your past to find out who hurt your inner child, you just have to acknowledge your emotions. You have to admit they are activated. You can then let go of how they affect you and get past them.

Most coaches and authors focus on thinking and behavior because it seems more tangible. We are a lot more aware of our thoughts than our emotions. Emotions are out of our everyday awareness. They are illusive. They are subtle and ever-changing. Thoughts drift through our minds like complete sentences from an internal voice, but emotions dangle in the background and color all of those thoughts like filters. Because of that, we don't notice emotions as directly. They are similar to ultraviolet rays we can only see through prisms. We experience their effects, but struggle to observe them in our everyday lives.

The Unseen Balancing Act Guiding Your Actions

When I was a little kid, nine or ten years old, I distinctly remember getting frustrated by not understanding my math homework. I would be pouting, crying, complaining, and doing whatever I could to get out of doing it. Finally my patient mom would sit me down. She would have me simply read line by line what I was supposed to do. About the third or fourth line in, I would start giggling because it started making so much more sense. I was able to do the assignment easily after that.

I see this same sort of thing happen when I first explain this emotion dynamic to someone in person. I can usually tell when the "aha" moment arrives. It's like a tiny explosion—*boom!*—it goes off all at once. They suddenly realize their attempts to change their thoughts without addressing their emotions first can't ever be successful.

You don't even have to prove it to yourself because you experience it all the time. If you *do* want proof, though, there are a couple of ways you can find it. One is by observing infants. Babies don't yet possess formal thought or language. They simply do not have the cognitive abilities to "think" the way adults do. Their brains have not developed enough yet. At the same time, they are obviously experiencing emotions that are causing them to react.

Babies have five instinctual drives. Those drives are hunger, fear, the need to be cared for, comfort, and stimulation. Babies' instincts lead them toward direct and dramatic reactions they can't explain. They grow out of those primitive behaviors, of course. However, when their emotions get triggered, they engage those same reactive patterns. Their behavior matures, but the patterned reaction stays with them for life.

For a day-to-day example, think about what happens when you're interrupted by something unexpected and annoying. Leaf blowers and babies are great examples. Imagine sitting next to a crying infant on a plane. When you are excited about life, you're engaged, productive, and feel great. Your response to the crying baby might be to smile, try to distract them with a silly face, or empathize with the parent. But when you are stressed and already on edge, you focus on the baby as a distraction or an intrusion. You might get furious. You might even lash out at the already stressed parent.

In either case, the thoughts that come to you have already been determined by your emotional filter. What you're going to do, and even what you're going to think, are largely set in motion by your emotion filter.

I intentionally picked a small situation like that because it's one most of us can relate to. When we think a little bit bigger, though, we see how these emotion-to-thought patterns can stack on top of one another over time.

When your emotion filtration is in balance, you live in the present moment. Whether things are going your way or not, you're okay. You are proactive, energized, and focused on what's next. You feel in control of yourself and your life. You are open to whatever comes your way. Conversely, when your filtration system is out of balance, the wrong emotional state is filtering and influencing every thought that comes to your mind. That set of impressions colors everything around you, causing you to see threats and react to your stories or thoughts. You start identifying problems that might not exist in the real world. Do this for too long, and they start calling it anxiety.

In addressing the filter, I talk about three emotional states. The first is the *balanced* emotional state, which is where we all strive to be. It is a spiritual place of peace, joy, and fulfillment. It's the most powerful state. It's where all intentional motivating action is generated. When this balanced emotional state is filtering information, it helps you reach your goals and bring others along with you on the journey.

The second state I define as the *vulnerable raw emotional state*. We unconsciously receive information from a frightened perspective. It is the dark, scary storehouse of old experience you've collected from day one. When viewing the world through this filter, you may feel frightened and victimized. It's as if the world is controlling you. You are at the mercy of everyone and everything. You feel powerless to change your situation. You do not know how to exert influence over your life, other people, or your surroundings. Everyone views the world through this state from time to time. However, if you stay in this state, over time you feel more defeated and may become apathetic and even stop trying altogether because it can feel like nothing you do has any effect.

In the third emotional state, we view the world through our *protective filter*. The majority of our problems stem from using this emotional filter. It's everyone's default emotional state. We don't just view the world from here; this filter is almost glued to our eyeballs. We live in it 99 percent of the time. It is our critical factor. It's your guardian at the gate. This part of our mind protects us by examining all information from a threat assessment standpoint. Its sole focus is to find and interpret threats.

Unfortunately your protective filter is also like your space suit—you need it for your journey. Like a bomb-detecting dog, it searches everywhere for potential harm. It also keeps you from going into your store-house of past experience because it believes that place is full of explo-sives. Your protective filter tells you that you need to stay out of your storehouse because it's dangerous; there's nothing of value in there, and it's very dark and scary. A major lie it whispers to you is, "If you go in there, you'll never come out."

While using this protective filter, we tend to overthink everything. We try to stop ourselves from feeling. We exert too much force and become overly controlling. We are constantly calculating, interpreting, or trying to mitigate damage rather than listening. As we push back against our fearful emotions, we end up constantly creating strife and conflict. Other people get caught up in the struggle. This causes most of the friction in our relationships, whether business or personal.

Approaching the world through the protective filter or the vulner-able raw emotional state both result in extreme frustration. It is our protective filter, however, that creates the terrible stories about what we're going through. The protective filter constantly blames the raw emotional state for all our problems. In any case, the cycles repeat again and again. Staying stuck in either of the protective filter or the raw emo-tional state will slow or even derail the path to success.

I often work with business professionals who are obviously trying too hard. The issue doesn't have anything to do with their thinking; if anything, they are pumping themselves full of "positive thinking" messages and reminders. Their thinking is only a symptom. They are "grinding it out." Some of these grinders are making good progress; others, not so much. The real problem is deeper down. Their emotions are driving that grind, and it's intense. They overcompensate by focus-ing outside themselves as they desperately seek more control. They have convinced themselves that working harder is smarter. They engage in too much needless activity; they cross boundaries and exert pressure. Some get angry and can become aggressive like the Incredible Hulk. Others just focus on the hope that their grinding will pay off someday. They keep pushing and pushing until something happens.

On the other hand, a business professional approaching their work from a raw emotional state looks very different. They may appear to be lacking ambition, make excuses, or complain about how hard it is to get ahead. They either take ineffective action or simply don't take action. When a person believes that nothing they try will work, they often shut down and stop trying altogether. Obviously, this isn't helpful. It's another situation where their emotional filter completely stops effective, proactive, action-based thoughts from producing results. These people often end up settling for what they have, telling themselves, "It could be worse."

We will dial in on these behaviors more closely in future chapters. The takeaway for the moment is the realization that even the best ideas can't compete with activated raw emotions or the protective filter. If every thought that comes through our mind has been poisoned by our filter suggesting we aren't good enough or can't succeed, then we will twist or ignore any helpful notion that comes our way. Even if someone has the exact answer to our problem, and has proven it will work, we simply won't hear it. Instead, we'll absorb whatever concept our mind turns it into. We'll take our own bad advice and sabotage ourselves over and over. The brilliance of others will flow right past us to the next open mind.

You rarely ever see high-performing individuals struggling with these roadblocks. They have reached a point where they are in the flow of making decisions quickly and getting things done. These people have used the balanced intentional filter enough with themselves that their raw emotions no longer get in their way. They have learned from the brilliance of others. They can now tap into their own intuition and brilliance. They aren't getting caught in their protective filter and relying on their own bad advice. They aren't overthinking things. They aren't obsessed with their own thoughts, inadequacies, and self-doubts. They are operating from a desire for results, they consistently take good advice and put it to work.

How We Break Out of Destructive Patterns

The first step to overcoming any problem is admitting it exists. You, I, and billions of others want to think we are smart, rational beings. And we *are* smart. It's just that we are also emotional creatures who default to thinking that whatever is in our heads is accurate even when it isn't logical or profitable to do so. It sucks, but those are the facts.

If you want to argue this, deny this, or feel certain you can use manifestation or positive thinking to create the improvements you have been dreaming about in your life, put this book down. Go make your vision board with a picture of your dream house. Or visualize your spouse losing fifteen pounds, melting their love handles away in your mind.

Then, when that doesn't work, come back and start reading again.

The traditional ways of thinking about motivation will definitely pump you up. They will definitely make you feel better, but it lasts only for a limited amount of time. They are the mental equivalent of bandages. To permanently break out of the traps you have set, you must perform a different sort of action.

Most people are not willing enough to move out of their comfort zones, but that's what it takes. You have to make a firm commitment to yourself that you are the person who will do what's necessary **no matter what** because you want more in your life. You must recognize, once and for all, that the problem doesn't start or end with your conscious thoughts. Even more importantly, you have to stick to your commitment to generating real, lasting change for yourself.

It's important to get that out of the way early. In the coming chapters I'll show you how you can use the power of action coupled with emotional identification to be more intentional in everything you do. In the process, I'm going to give you the tools you need to get past the bottlenecks in your personal and professional lives. However, you have to be honest with yourself, open to some new ideas, and willing to challenge your own assumptions. You have to be willing to do things a little (or maybe a lot) differently than you have in the past if you truly want to be a high performer.

Whether you are just getting started or an established executive who feels like you are running out of space to grow, the issues are the same. So I invite you to follow along with me regardless of where you are in your life, your relationships, or your career. Commit now to approaching the material with rigorous self-honesty and an open mind. In return I'll show you exactly how to break out of whatever rut you might find yourself in.

It all starts with shutting down the lie machine that sits on top of your shoulders. We will tackle that in the next chapter, and I will introduce the amazingly simple process I use.

CHAPTER 3

Your Brain's Broken Filtration System

Here is the plain and simple truth: your mind is feeding you useless lies. Those lies lead to actions that sabotage you and hold you back. The logical solution would be to change those thoughts. But that takes you back to the big problem you started with, which is that you aren't really aware of the unconscious emotional filters coloring your thoughts in the first place. So, any conscious effort to change your thinking will be temporary at best and ineffective for the long run.

To get to the root of the problem, you have to focus on your emotional filtration. Imagine a filtration system between your emotions and your thinking that lets the ideas that conform to your existing perceptions through and eliminates all else. Imagine the filter as a water filter for a moment. Although water is going through the filter and is affected by that process, we only see the end product. We cannot see the filtration. We cannot change the filtration process by covering up the water spout. The water just builds up and eventually sprays everywhere. The water has still been filtered the same way.

It's important to remember that this filtration is all perfectly normal and natural. For the great majority of us, it's not the sign of a mental issue or a brain disease. It's not the product of trauma or a turbulent childhood, even if you have suffered horrible traumas. It doesn't mean that we are broken or defective. Those are just examples of the filter doing its job and the beliefs that are created from the filter needing to be cleaned. It's simply what our minds do to protect us from what scares us and we generally don't like or understand. Much of the mental health issue are resolved when this filtration is fixed. I have helped hundreds of people transform through this process. They left diagnoses, medications, and therapy behind.

How does it work? Well, every one of the sensations that comes to us from the outside world is noticed on some level. All the sights, sounds, smells, touches, and ideas floating around out there bombard us throughout the day. Obviously, our brain can't process them all; it has to organize and prioritize. The easiest way to do this is by allowing anything that makes sense or causes us "happiness" to pass through the balanced intentional or "no big deal" filter or "nonthreat" filter. We're able to talk about and explore any of that stuff. However, it doesn't get our attention because it is not really a threat, even if it could be useful.

On the other hand, any sensation that scares us or concerns us will go through the protective filter. Our protective filter turns on, like a red alert on *Star Trek* and we become critical and react as we predict all possible danger.

Now, imagine a picture book from your early childhood, opened up to the middle. You might find a backyard scene filled with all kinds of little animals—cats, dogs, squirrels, and birds. On the page, you're asked to search for all the cats. As you start looking, you *also* begin filtering out all the other animals and zero in on the felines. You may even mistake some other animals for cats because you're so intent on looking for them.

This is an easy way to understand filtering. Its effects are bigger and last longer than you might expect. For instance, if this were a real experiment or study, you would likely keep noticing cats wherever you went for the rest of your day. You had already trained your unconscious mind to find them, so it would. It's also interesting that if guns were hidden in the same picture, your protective filter would likely take over. It would begin detecting the guns and toss aside the cute kitties, instead focusing on the perceived threat. We may likely realize that we switched to guns, but our protective filter will rationalize that we chose to switch as quickly as when we noticed the first gun.

If your prevailing emotional filter is one of worry, panic, and defeat, then every bit of news you hear will reinforce that perception. How can it not, when you're already looking for it? The things that might point toward happiness or success will simply get filtered out. You will be left with exactly what you expected. Then you will tell yourself a story in split seconds to make sense of your action so that you stay congruent. This is the old adage life goes where you focus.

A Never-Ending Cycle of Fear

The interesting and troubling thing about the emotional filter is that its results multiply over time. The filter reinforces itself through a very simple process.

What happens if we wake up feeling unusually anxious? For all the reasons I've explained, it's very likely that whatever happens during the day will set us even more on edge. We're going to perceive risks and threats everywhere, even if they aren't apparent to other people. The important thing, though, is that the cycle won't just continue—it will actually spiral down.

When we're scared, the world seems scary. That causes us to see scary things. The more scary things we see, the scarier the world becomes. So, if we start in a place of fear at the beginning of one day, we're likely going to be even *more anxious* the next day. This can go on and on just out of our awareness for years until we're strung out on medications and feel like we can't face even the simplest challenges or obstacles.

While I'm using the example of fear, the same thing can happen with other emotions. A lack of self-worth (feelings of worthlessness) gives us another easy illustration.

> Wendell (a fictional person) feels worthless or "less than" others. He begins to act accordingly. Wendell shows up that way. He actually invites people, unknowingly, to treat him that way through his conversation and behavior. That leads to the very failure and bad treatment by friends, family members, and coworkers that Wendell fears. Is it any wonder, then, that Wendell begins to feel even more undervalued? Are we surprised that he continues to sink deeper into this cycle?

Emotional cycles almost always come back to fear because we fear feeling vulnerable raw emotions. We have all experienced these in one form or another throughout our lives. We have experienced the fear of intimacy, the fear of failure, the fear of success, and the fear of being found out. We fear that others won't like us. Or, if they *do* like us, we fear that they'll stop. We are afraid we won't measure up, that our loved ones will be harmed, or that we will die. The list goes on and on and on.

Automatic thinking is reactive. It is so good at coming up with these fears that it will keep doing so at a nonstop rate if we don't address it. On some level of evolutionary thinking, going back to caveman times, it makes sense. It can help us to physically survive in dangerous environments. At the same time, though, it's an ineffective habit that can keep us stuck in place. It makes us unhappy at best. More often it makes us downright miserable, stopping us from pursuing our vision. This is where the mindset movement jumps in and says, "Just change your thinking and you will succeed." However, this is like thinking that if we change the nozzle on a paint sprayer, it will change the color of the paint.

I like to tell new clients that I am so devoted to my framework for change because I know it transforms lives, and that's true. However, there is another side to the coin: if you don't face up to your fears and emotions, they will ruin you. You must change the color of the paint to spray a different color.

People often talk about wearing rose-colored glasses. They say life gets better and better if you see hope and possibilities everywhere. But when you're walking around wearing dirty, dingy goggles, you'll only see crap wherever you look. In fact, searching for signs of progress or improvement won't help because you simply won't see what's right in front of you. I am a fan of clear glasses and putting in the effort to really see yourself clearly.

When you approach a problem, or just life in general, from the vulnerable raw place of fear, there's nowhere to go but down. The cycle will repeat itself again and again, with the only difference being that you'll feel worse and more discouraged each time. This might not be a popular idea. In fact, nobody wants to admit this idea, but look around and ask yourself whether you can really argue with it.

Albert Einstein once said that the eighth wonder of the world was compounding interest. Perhaps the greatest thinker of all time marveled at the way results can build on each other. If he had been a psychologist instead of a physicist, though, he might have emphasized that it also works the same way with our lives and our emotions.

How a Bad Day Becomes a Bad Life

I bet you're starting to get a good sense of the way our emotional filtering works. To get the full picture, I want to move past the mechanism and peek at its effects. In other words, I want to share a picture of what it looks like in the real world.

Healthy, high-achieving people are in what I call a balanced intentional state. They are in touch with their emotional selves. They aren't ignoring any warning signs or going overboard with their reactions. They can focus on bigger goals. They are productive and happily make progress, because they feel in tune with themselves and the world. They have a positive, growth-oriented self-concept. They live in faith that things will work out. They sense they are in control of their own destiny.

The rest of the world is continually being overwhelmed by one emotion or another, several if not all of them at the same time. This happens in one of two ways. Either the raw emotions are flooded or the protective filter is busy helping us avoid our raw emotions.

To be clear, the raw emotional state simply means that our mindset is being flooded with strong emotion (like fear or powerlessness). The protective emotional filter, on the other hand, is attempting to overcorrect for the same kind of strong emotion using our mindset. So, revisiting our friend Wendell, when he feels dominated by his raw emotions and experiences, he will fear being excluded. He will likely count himself out before anyone else can. In a social gathering he will be passive and quiet. He may avoid going out all together to avoid pain he believes he might feel. Over time he develops a protective story that he doesn't like to socialize or that he even has social anxiety. But in reality he's reacting to his raw emotions.

Now if Wendell is protecting himself from his raw emotions, he will try to control of that unconscious fear. He will either try to take over and take center stage, or he might act as if he doesn't want relationships at all. They are two sides of the same problem, and neither one is in balance.

It's easy to spot someone who feels completely dominated by raw emotions. These are the victims of the world. We've all seen them. We all probably know one. Some of us may even be one. These victims are convinced that they have to settle for what they have, and they tell themselves it could be worse. They believe that the world is a miserable and difficult place and there isn't much of anything they can do to change it. They are easy to identify because they complain a lot, make excuses, and have essentially given up on improving themselves or their circumstances.

Someone who is being partially dominated by their raw emotions might recognize that there is a problem in their life, but they keep fighting against it. In fact, these individuals are often clients of mine. They still have the idea that life is hard, but they won't give up. They start businesses and trudge along, feeling discouraged because it's hard and full of sacrifices. They have an insight that something is wrong, and that it has to do with themselves, but they still feel stuck and don't know how to move forward. Many of these people start justifying and rationalizing that they are happy where they are at. They do this because they don't know how to grow toward that next level, whether it is business or personal.

Other individuals lean more toward using their protective filter. Typically, these folks are high achievers, but they beat themselves up. They feel a lot of internal pressure despite their accomplishments. They cannot celebrate any wins because they believe these weren't warranted. Their filter tells them that they are not good enough. They want to be successful and feel worthy, but they struggle to shed harmful internal chatter. I know this group well, too, because they show up in my coaching programs every month. The funny thing is that whether they are making under six figures or over seven figures, this group all tortures themselves about their performance.

All the way at the other end of the spectrum, we find individuals who are completely consumed in their protective filter. You can spot them right away because they're cocky, entitled, and prone to doing things that just aren't socially and sometimes even ethically acceptable. They may find a lot of material success, but they talk much bigger than they truly are. They usually hop from one job or career to the next because they use up resources and people can't stand them. These people typically are not coachable.

If you aren't sure where you sit on the spectrum, consider the way you talk to yourself and others. Here are some things you might hear people in each of these categories say:

- *Completely flooded by raw emotions: "It will never work. Nothing I do is ever good enough. There's no point in trying. Nothing works out for me."*
- *Partially overwhelmed by raw emotions: "Things are hard. I just can't seem to do it. If I could just catch a break. I wish things weren't so tough for me. It's exhausting. I just need some good prospects."*
- *Partially protective filter: "Someday this will work out for me. If I could just do it right. If I just learn more, or try harder, someday I'll succeed."*
- *Completely protective filter: "People are sheep and deserve what they get. I have to get mine before everyone else gets theirs. Take care of number one. It's you or me."*

In my experience, people at extreme ends of the spectrum are rare. These people are essentially uncoachable unless they make a huge effort to shift. They must be willing to become self-aware and then open themselves to connecting to their unconscious emotions to have more wonderful things in life. The vast majority of us, however, fall somewhere in the middle when we aren't in balance. Thankfully, all of us can see fast and permanent improvement once we adopt the strategy and techniques I'm going to share.

Repairing Your Broken Filter

Any filtration system needs regular maintenance. If your emotional filter is clogged, then it needs to be repaired or replaced. Contrary to popular belief, this doesn't have to involve a huge, painstaking process that takes decades of therapy. You just have to follow an intentional game plan.

Recognizing your own tendency toward certain emotional states and altering them is well worth the effort. It's one of the few things that can actually live up to the label of "dramatic, life-changing, or transformational." Not only do you get better results when you are in emotional balance, but you feel a lot more joyful and more fulfilled, too. Balanced intentional people don't feel overwhelmed. They don't become flooded by feelings of powerlessness or fear rejection. They are confident, courageous, and intentional. When they do get knocked off balance, they know how to identify their raw emotions and return to using their balanced intentional filter.

With that in mind, let's move to the next chapter and see what we can do to stop reinforcing fear and other unhelpful emotional states.

CHAPTER 4

Fixing the Filter

It's a daunting prospect to realize that you have an unconscious filter that keeps you stuck in a ring of fire.

The protective filter constantly causes you to ignore or sabotage your opportunities, which is also bleak. The idea that your thinking is actually used to hide your fears and lie to yourself can be absolutely alarming. The result for most of us is that we end up focusing on what isn't working. We end up spending all our time explaining why we can't do things rather than taking action. This is absolutely discouraging. So, if that's the case, why even try to improve yourself?

Obviously pointing out how much you live in your protective filter is not the takeaway I want you to have from reading this book. You do, however, have to understand the problem to make any real progress. I've focused on the harmful aspects of your filter to this point because I want you to really understand just how destructive listening to your own lies can be.

Of course, that isn't the end of the story. In fact, it's just the beginning. When you're balanced, you don't just feel focused or energized—you have an enormous advantage over everyone else. While others are mired in the muck of doubt and second-guessing, you are free from that dead weight. At that point, you can boost your own productivity, enhance your relationships, and be a lot more effective in helping others. You can live a fulfilling life of high performance the way it was meant to be enjoyed.

In this chapter we are going to put you on that path. It starts now with identifying your emotions in a helpful way.

Emotions—What's the Use?

The standard model of self-improvement these days is to "think better thoughts and minimize negative emotions." This sounds great and can definitely help gurus sell a lot of books, but for the vast majority of people, it just doesn't work.

I've already covered some problems with positive thinking as a change technique. It boils down to the fact that we have only limited control over our thoughts and emotions. Remember the lie machine? That's really the protective filter. The number-one lie it tells us is that we can control our thinking and emotions.

Even if that weren't the case, and we could control our thinking, the positive thinking technique would come up short. That's because it revolves around the superstitious idea that we need to avoid certain words like cracks in the sidewalk or even stop feeling painful things because they might take us off our game. The notion that we need to avoid pain or negative emotions is wrong and weak in itself. It is ridiculous to think that because you use certain words, you will program yourself for failure. In fact, the words you use are important to say because they are symptoms of the emotional state you are in or the emotional filter you are seeing the world through.

Emotions are not just useful. They are necessary to keep us alive and interested in life. One of the biggest reasons we get confused about emotions and avoid them is the idea that we have negative emotions. Negative emotions do not exist.

Why do I say this? When you realize that the labels *positive* and *negative* don't actually apply very well to emotions, everything changes.

Emotions are simply emotions. It's actually the protective filter identifying emotions as negative. It is much more honest to say that when we feel our raw emotion, we don't like the emotion or the raw emotions are unpleasurable. When we're using our protective filter, we feel better than when we're dominated by our raw emotions, but we are still uneasy and off balance.

The gurus often teach that there are four basic emotions: glad, sad, mad, and scared. My model of the mind identifies a full twenty-seven. Even if we consider the real range of sensations, though, the bigger truth is obscured. It's not about what we're feeling, but whether we're balanced, because when we are out of emotional balance our emotions control us. It's only when we are rigorously honest with ourselves that we experience that balanced, intentional state and start to feel clean joy, clean sorrow, and clean pleasure.

A few weeks ago, two of my dear friends experienced a tragedy. Their young adult child passed away from a terminal illness. They are experiencing what I call clean sorrow. They miss their daughter dearly and feel the deep grief. The difference for them is that they are able to identify their raw emotions. They have no regrets in their relationship. There was nothing left unsaid. They have truly accepted her passing, although they feel hurt and disappointed that it had to happen.

Every pain has a purpose. If you put your hand on a hot stove, it's going to hurt like hell. At the same time, though, you're going to learn a valuable lesson.

On a more humorous note, when she was about four, my sister once put a penny in an electrical socket. She got the shock of a lifetime. She actually shot back a couple of feet and started crying. She made that mistake exactly one time. Most children do things like this and then learn quickly to avoid similar sorts of hurt in the future.

In that way, so-called "negative" emotions such as shame, jealousy, and hurt can help us to grow. At the very least, they can prevent us from inflicting unnecessary damage on our bodies and minds. It hurts to feel raw emotions like shame and rejection, but they also bring valuable lessons. If we seek to shut them off or limit them or avoid them, we end up stunting our own development. When we acknowledge them and see them for what they are, raw emotions motivate us to seek connection, reparation, and forgiveness for any damage we have done, and we forgive any damage done to us. Raw emotions also serve as effective boundaries that we can share with others to help them know how to treat us.

For example, if you say something stupid in public and then feel embarrassed about it, the end result might be that you consider your words more carefully next time. This is helpful social development. If you replay the same event in your head, however, it creates a useless spiral that serves no purpose. When you view the world through the balanced intentional filter, the emotions are useful. When you view the world through your raw emotions or protective filter, your emotion becomes useless, burdensome, or even abusive and detrimental.

It is so common to replay our mistakes that there is a term for it: emotional spirals. These spirals are created when an event triggers our emotion and we dwell on that interaction. We then replay the event again and again like a movie in our mind. We cannot seem to move on or take any useful action. The net result is that our self-esteem crumbles as we move lower and lower into a flooded raw emotional state. We begin falling down one emotional rabbit hole after another.

Take shame as another example. When we continually feel shame, it's debilitating. If we feel like we aren't good enough, or that we're broken or defective and the world is against us, that's going to prevent us from putting ourselves out there. Once we're at that point, all the "positive thinking" in the world won't help, and trying to avoid the raw emotion isn't the answer. In many cases, positive thinking strategies just make us feel more like we are lying to ourselves. Instead of creating more confidence, we eat away at our own trust and belief in ourselves as we use those suggested affirmations. The only way to break this cycle is to face up to what's going on in our unconscious emotional mind.

We simply cannot ignore our raw emotions. We cannot pretend that they aren't there and hope they'll go away. We certainly cannot will them away. Our raw emotions serve a purpose. They are *real*; the stories that emanate from the emotions are illusions, but our raw emotions are essential to our life. They simply aren't *useful* to us when we protect ourselves from them, ignore them, or try to dominate them. That's why, if you truly want growth or change, you need to admit your raw emotions and bring them into the light to move you back into balance.

It's worth noting, by the way, that the same thing can happen with so-called "positive" emotions. Yes, we want to feel proud of ourselves. We want to feel powerful. We want to feel confident and experience pleasure. Many times our protective filter takes over and tries to manufacture what we think we should feel. If we go overboard in trying to find those positive emotions, we're only going to throw the rest of our life off center. A person who chases the feeling of achievement for the sole purpose of proving they can do it is like someone who tries to self-medicate with chocolate bars. Both are going to get a short-term high followed by a deeper crash, often accompanied by an unhealthy amount of self-harm and self-loathing upon failure—i.e., the deal falling through or the unintended weight gain.

Cleaning Your Filter Once and for All

Identifying your raw emotions or cleaning out the storehouse is the only way to clean the filter. Your protective filter has clouded your perception since the beginning of your thought life. This clog in your filter influences every situation in your life. The protective filter wants to stay in control because it believes it is the only thing keeping you safe. You cannot filter emotions into the useful category until you stop the interpretation and assumptions of the protective filter. Only then can you engage in clear thinking, infinite imagination, recognize useful ideas, and act upon them effectively.

Once the protective filter is cleaned, you can begin to learn and grow. You can take in the true meaning of lessons you learn, and you can generate a more fulfilling future. If you are reading this book because you want to find a sense of peace and control, then my advice is to follow the suggestions in this book. Stop ignoring and avoiding your raw emotions; when you identify them, it allows you to clean out your storehouse. You can then begin to live through your balanced intentional emotional filter.

Instructions to Clean Our Filter

The first step in cleaning the filter is to examine the information going through the filter. At first this seems difficult, but it is as easy as taking inventory in a store. Focus on seeing what is going through your protective filter.

Start examining your thinking by simply writing down a list of the names of people in your life who upset you. Next to the name, write up to ten words describe the event. That's it.

In a new column, write a list of how you think you were affected in the areas of self-esteem, safety, ambition, and relationships. What have you told yourself about what others think about you? How did you tell yourself when you felt threatened? How did it affect your ambition? (Did the event make you want to try harder or make you want to quit?) How did you see your relationship with these individuals based on the interaction?

In the next column, write down what you did as a result of what you told yourself in the previous column. What did you do to change how the other person saw you? What did you do to ensure your safety? What action did you take—did you try harder or quit . . . or both? What did you do to change the relationship based on your thinking?

Finally, we examine the causes and conditions. Each of the raw emotions triggered some thought or story that you acted on to cause yourself a problem. Now you'll examine how each of your raw emotions triggered the protective filter in this incident.

You only need to inventory a few of these events because we are pattern people. We use the same patterns based on what we protect ourselves from. Once we see the pattern and the raw emotion that triggered the thinking, we let go of the need to protect ourselves. We become much more balanced and intentional because our filter is clean.

Once you finish this inventory, it's important to discuss it with someone else. None of us have the ability to see our own blind spots. We don't see where we are still lying to ourselves. As you discover your patterns and mistakes, you can correct them. You can be effective; you can be powerful. You see who you truly are and can be. At this point, you can start having the effect on the world the way you've always wanted to. You can get on with the business of life and live based on results instead of on "what ifs" and interpretations.

It's All in the Results You Achieve

Imagine for a moment that one of your best friends decided to earn his or her pilot's license. To celebrate this great achievement, the two of you decide to go on a trip to your favorite golf resort, beach town, or Alpine ski village.

The morning of the trip, you pack a bag and meet your friend at the airport. The weather is perfect, and you are impressed with the way your friend handles the aircraft, performing the takeoff and landing like a true professional. The flight is smooth and stress-free. And yet, once you step off the plane, you realize you've come to a destination that was hundreds of miles in the wrong direction. How would you feel about your friend's skills as an aviator?

While this is a silly story, it almost perfectly sums up the way many individuals approach self-improvement. In fact, it's something I have seen again and again in the personal/professional development industry. Men and women will come to see me knowing that something needs to change, all the while flying off in the wrong direction, fighting off the advice or self-realizations that could make all the difference. Instead they opt for a shiny object that sounds great and is marketed well. They are soon let down again.

Let's be very clear: when you are convinced that everything you're doing in your life and career is correct, but you aren't getting the results you want, then you are missing the obvious. Focusing on the future, hoping that things will turn around, is a bad plan. Believing that someday your current strategy will start working is just plain stupid. Engaging in the same behaviors that don't work again and again will not yield different results; they will only leave you with raw emotions and a sense of being broken. As Einstein said, "Insanity is doing the same thing over and over but expecting different results."

I have coached so many people who weren't making the kind of money they wanted to make. They weren't hitting that next level they wanted. They weren't lacking energy or ambition. Several were busy to the point of feeling overwhelmed with their schedules and commitments. The one thing all of them had in common, though, is that while they might have been hardworking experts in some area, they clearly were not experts in growing their businesses. They weren't just taking their own bad advice—they were sticking to it.

This isn't just illogical, it's incredibly frustrating. It's difficult for them, for all of the people depending on them, and especially for those who care about them. I bet you know *exactly* what I'm referring to. How many times has a friend or family member come to you with some sort of problem and then refused to follow the proposed solution you offered? Or worse, how many dismissed your advice saying they know or shooting your idea down before even trying it . . . professing that the suggestion you offered wouldn't work. Even worse, it was clear to both of you that you knew more about the subject than they did. How many times have *you* been in the position of ignoring or even dismissing the good advice someone else had to offer?

We can't turn this human tendency off just by wishing it away. There is no magic phrase that will suddenly stop us from following ourselves down the wrong paths over and over. What I can do, though, is give an easy way to stop listening to yourself: *Just pay attention to what you are and aren't getting from your own life.* That will tell you exactly what our priorities are and whether you are committed to the right answer or just *your* own answer.

You can't tune out the noise and make your emotional filter work while simultaneously thinking you are the smartest and wisest person in the world. Reality doesn't work that way. If you haven't had the financial success you are looking for, then you aren't doing things that will make you rich. If you are overweight, then your approach to fitness isn't as sharp as it could be. When your business lacks for customers, then you have to get honest about your weaknesses in lead generation, sales ability, or closing skills.

The results always tell the truth, even if our minds rarely ever do. If you aren't where you want to be in some important aspect of your life, then it's time to break your attachment to the stories, thoughts, and actions that have led you to this point. It's time to put results into action with your emotions.

Continued Monitoring of Your Emotional Filter

All of us have (and need) an emotional filter. What is most unhelpful is to allow yourself to dwell on raw emotions and memories again and again. The fact that you are not getting the results you want in your life should be proof enough.

After you complete your inventory, the next step is to shift from using your ineffective protective filter and be able to see things from our balance intentional filter. We have a map of sorts showing us how we protect ourselves. To keep using this filter, you must continue to identify the raw emotions the same way you did in our inventory. The more you practice this inventory process, the better and the longer you stay using the balanced intentional filter and the more effective you'll be.

A word of caution: It is very easy to slip back into the protective filter without knowing it. Results are the key to knowing which filter you are working from. It is much easier to return to using the balanced intentional filter when you continue to monitor your results.

You'll be more aware of your patterns, so it is much easier to identify the thoughts and impressions you should or shouldn't trust. You can now see your own stories in a different light. It is much easier to be discerning from the balanced intentional perspective.

Now is a perfect time to start introducing other viewpoints into your life. Instead of relying on your own bad advice, start to get feedback from those who have better information and can put your best interests at heart.

It is impossible for any of us to analyze ourselves in the same way that a true friend or an impartial colleague can do. Even now, after many years of schooling and clinical experience, I am still quite capable of going down my own rabbit holes. No one is immune. Sometimes our overthinking causes us to go overboard and focus too much on a bad idea that we think is amazing. Sometimes we hesitate on ideas instead of pulling the trigger.

We all stray from reality at times. Our imagination can also move us toward absolute genius. However, when we act on any of it without a solid outside opinion, we open ourselves to horrendous mistakes. I have valued every penny and every moment I have spent on my coaches and mentors because, while I have many moments of brilliance, I also have blind spots. My coaches and mentors reel me back in. They keep me on my path. They encourage bold moves, and they shorten the time it takes to reach my goals.

This topic of drawing help from others is one we will return to several times in the coming chapters. For now, just realize that it's a crucial part of maintaining your balanced intentional filter. All of us are prone to following patterns that feel familiar and safe, even if they lead to destruction in our personal and professional lives. Breaking out of them isn't difficult, but it takes work and dedication. However, the commitment is to a better life for yourself, and the payoff can be enormous.

CHAPTER 5

Learning to Trust Yourself

The realization that everything we think is tainted by the protective filter (i.e., the lie machine) is destabilizing at first. Many people prefer to argue against that idea, put their heads back in the sand, and pretend that this is just not so. That's actually the filter doing its job. Funny enough, a lot of the cognitive therapists and mindset coaches fall into this group. We all confuse behavior, thinking, and emotion. These concepts have been taught wrong for years, whether in the general public or even much of higher education.

When I was in grad school, one of my professors pulled me aside when I was talking about a client "feeling" angry. I never made that mistake again. She made the point that anger was a behavior. She went on to say that anger is a common behavioral reaction to feeling the emotion of powerlessness. She explained to me that emotion is our unconscious internal experience of the world. Behavior, on the other hand, is conscious observable action. We can see anger in their body language, verbal language, and tone. This means that we can see our behavior and know about it. Thinking is nothing more than an internal behavior. We can see people thinking. Because our emotion is unconscious, we mistakenly mislabel behavior as emotion and confuse our communication. This was a valuable lesson that helped immensely in my understanding of where people become stuck and how to help them get moving.

Understanding these facts is very useful and can be a catalyst for positive change. At first, in terms of our linear day-to-day life, it can be tough to start questioning the very thinking that has kept us alive for all these years. But if nothing our protective filter tells us is real or genuine, then why make an effort at all?

As a practical matter, we have to be able to trust our own mind or at least know how to correct the errors our lie machine is feeding us. It's not nearly as impossible as it sounds. However, it does require an ongoing effort and practice.

The tough thing about change—especially inner change—is that it requires continuous work. It gets a whole lot easier over time, but it's an ongoing process of recognizing our raw emotions in order to move to our balanced intentional filter. We can identify the raw emotions that trigger us to create our own lies, mistakes, and misinterpretations. We can start to see ourselves much more clearly.

At first, it sounds like hard work. It is not usually something anyone wants to hear. This is really not a difficult or arduous process at all; we just don't like doing it. We all have a lazy side to us that just wants to have the work done once and be done with it. Most would prefer to think they're going to find the right guru, book, or mentor who will magically solve the problem for them overnight. Those dramatic shifts can work for a day or two, but it takes more to redirect the path of a lifetime. Remember, if you aren't getting the results you want, it's an indication you haven't put enough effort in the right areas for a long enough time.

I wanted to start this chapter with this point because change can be gradual right up to the point where it isn't. To the outside observer, success looks like it occurs suddenly, all at once. The person who has been grinding away for weeks, months, or years knows better.

You may feel as if your life isn't all it could be at the moment. Until now you probably haven't had a good idea why, if only because most of the processes that cause you to doubt, delay, and fail are unconscious. This is your chance to go all in and make a change.

You Don't Know What You Don't Know

An old fish swims up to a pair of younger fish and says: "Nice day, fellas—how's the water?" The younger fish look baffled, and then one responds: "Where is this water?" The young fish then swim off in search of the water.

This is a silly little story, but I have always liked it. Most of us are exactly like the young fish. We think what we are experiencing is reality, completely unaware of the filters that influence what we see and feel. Our perceptions are so thick that they just become part of our surroundings. In fact, it can take something pretty shocking to snap us into a state of realization.

In the world of psychology, we refer to this as unconscious bias. It means having filters, perceptions, or even blind spots we aren't aware of.

By coincidence, unconscious bias has become a huge topic in the media as this is being written. All across North America, and even the world, citizens are protesting the unequal treatment of racial minorities. And some of us are being asked to consider whether we have unhelpful attitudes we haven't even been aware of.

I'm not going to wade deeply into that discussion here because it's outside the scope of this book, but unconscious bias is a real thing. Studies have shown again and again that we aren't just influenced by preconceived notions about the world around us, but we can also be easily overwhelmed by them.

For a very simple illustration of the way this works, consider what happens when a sports star or political figure finds himself or herself in trouble. You can almost predict how people will react to the situation based on their prior affiliations. If they were fans of the player or the team or members of the same political party, they likely will be quick to minimize the behavior, try to justify it, or dismiss it as a one-off incident. If they were already rivals, then the experience will simply reinforce the belief that the other team or organization is filled with bad apples.

Remember, in these instances we are all hearing the same news. The facts aren't different for each side; only the interpretation changes. Once again, I'm not going to dwell on the political or sociological aspects of the problem here. Instead, I want you to explore how your unconscious biases might color the way you feel about yourself or other people and situations in the world.

When I worked in corrections, the guards would try to hand me files for a new inmate assigned to my unit. They would do whatever they could to get me to read the file before I saw the inmate. I would refuse because I wanted to have as unbiased an experience of the new guy as I could. The guy was in prison, so he was already fighting an uphill battle. I was not going to make it worse by reading all the drama of how bad he was on paper. I found I got much further and developed better relationships with the inmates when I let them tell me who they were.

We all have unconscious biases that affect the way we see others and even ourselves. What are you telling yourself about the world at large? What are you telling yourself about your business? What are you telling yourself about the money you're making? How is it different from what you're telling yourself about the money highly successful people are making? What are you telling yourself about health or about relationships?

The One Question You Must Always Ask

There is a simple way to break the cycle put in place by your unconscious filters and biases. Notice I said *simple,* not *easy.* It involves asking
yourself this question again and again:

"How am I wrong about this?"

This is the most important question, the one you should *always* ask.
You should then also ask:

"How else am I wrong?"
"How am I mistaken?"
"What else am I missing?"

"How am I wrong about this?" was the simple question that I used
with the young man who believed he had some mysterious disease.

In any given situation where you are upset, angry, or fearful, simply
ask yourself, "How am I wrong about this?" Don't ask if you *could* be
wrong, or how someone else might see it. Just assume for a moment
your position isn't the right one and try to find out how you are wrong.

In *Hamlet,* Shakespeare had Polonius tell his son, "This above all:
To thine own self be true . . ."

When we are seeking to discover how we might be wrong about a
situation, we take a much more objective position. This is the same position scientists take in attempting to disprove hypotheses. When we begin
by assuming that our theories are incorrect and seek to prove our mistakes, it makes it a lot easier to find them. When we look for those flaws,
we have much more success in growing and changing. When we try to
prove we are right, we become rigid and create strife, drama, and trauma.

This can be more difficult than we tend to realize. Most of us don't want to be wrong. We are deeply invested into our own positions, and we hate the idea that we could be responsible for our own misery. It triggers all of the raw emotions around inferiority, worthlessness, and shame. However, admitting our fault is nearly always the first step toward personal responsibility and improving our situation. It also amazingly does exactly the opposite of what we fear. We fear others will think poorly of us and see us as inferior. The reality is that people will tend to have more respect for us. They will appreciate us more. They will tend to give us more latitude and listen to our perspective more when we admit our errors.

Not long ago, one of my clients called me in the middle of the day. He was dealing with a relatively mundane request from his wife and had hard feelings about it. She had asked him to pick up their dog up from the vet even though he already had a busy workday. The real problem, he believed, was that his wife was constantly bombarding him with these sorts of last-minute requests.

To hear him explain it, his issues were actually quite valid. He had plenty to do, and it didn't seem reasonable that she should be piling more on his plate. Still, I asked him to consider all of the ways he might be wrong.

My client was reluctant to engage in this line of thinking at first, but once he did, after a few expletives, several ideas came to mind. Perhaps his wife was also busy because of an unforeseen issue at her job. Maybe she thought because he was closer to the vet, and generally had a more flexible schedule, it would be easier for him to pick up the dog. Perhaps it was more comfortable for him because the dog was more receptive to his direction than hers. Or maybe she just appreciated having such a supportive partner who could handle details like this on the fly.

Until the magic question was asked, my client didn't even consider any of that. We all do this. We make up our own stories and have one-sided conversations with ourselves. We skip talking to the others in our lives and then wonder why they don't see things our way.

Who was right and who was wrong? I'm not really sure, but I know that the conversation they had that night was a lot more productive than they would have had if he hadn't stopped to consider other perspectives. And I know that in both my personal life and my professional life, I see that asking "How am I wrong about this?" nearly always creates a curiosity in me that searches for better answers. These answers lead to dramatic realizations and produce better businesses, better marriages, and better conversations. Those are the kinds of results we are looking for.

What Are Your Possibilities?

At first when you realize you are wrong about a great many things, the ground might feel unstable, as though you were experiencing an ongoing earthquake. However, something almost magical happens when you begin to question your own ideas and assumptions. You move past the rigid closed loop of your own protective mindset. You become willing and open to imagine other perspectives. Even if those new ideas and assumptions don't end up ringing true, it's a creative thinking exercise that will usually lead you in a fresh and valuable direction.

Robert Schuller, a popular preacher in the 1990s, wrote a book called *Move Ahead with Possibility Thinking*. He said, "The only place where your dream becomes impossible is in your own thinking." When you focus on the challenges and conflicts in your life, they begin to consume you. They become bigger and bigger weeds in your imagination as we tend to them like flowers.

Another way to engage this part of your mind is to ask, "What are the possibilities?" When you specifically challenge your own assumptions about your problems, along with the facts you might believe are solid, this simple question is invaluable. Other useful questions include:

"What other possibilities could potentially be true about this situation or this person?"

"What are the next steps to move me forward?"

"What positive motivations might other people have in dealing with or helping me?"

"Is there a chance that the situation isn't as bad, as good, as straightforward, or as one-dimensional as I think?"

Along the same lines, another of my favorites regarding hard feelings toward others is: "How is this serving me?" In other words, what are you really getting out of this grudge or this disagreement? More often than not, the answer is absolutely *nothing*. We spend so much time wasting tons of energy overthinking a situation, venting, and pulling others into our rabbit holes of frustration and resentment, for no real purpose. We create a dramatic time suck that takes everyone down with us.

When you ask yourself these tough questions, don't expect that your first answer is the correct one. When working with my clients, I often assume it's going to take several different attempts to get to the real honesty of an emotion.

For instance, I might ask a client: "Why are you angry about what happened?" They will typically give me a surface-level answer and point out what the other person did. They will become angry all over again as they describe the injustice they experienced.

This is actually because anger causes anger. Anger is really a behavior to help us fight against feelings of powerlessness. If I then ask my client about their feeling of powerlessness, I'll get a variation on the original theme. However, as I keep going, we will eventually reach a point where a deeper truth comes out. This will be apparent in a couple of ways. First there will be a more raw and unfiltered statement. They are now talking about themselves and not the others involved. My client then often actually experiences a physical shift as they listen to what they've said.

You can try this on your own. Stop and think about the last argument you had with a loved one and ask yourself why it upset you so much. Your first thought will likely be something that was said or done that caused you to be upset. Keep looking for different answers. Eventually you will reach a deeper truth, such as, "I felt powerless over that person seeing my side of the conversation." Or "I felt invalidated, like my feelings didn't matter when they didn't listen." Once you frame things in this light, it gets much easier to let go of the emotion, let go of the resentment, deal with the miscommunication, and simply move on.

Few problems are ever as big as we make them out to be. And even when they are, we can't find the solutions without identifying our own raw emotions in a way that goes beyond a behavioral reaction. More importantly, when become better at identifying our own raw emotions, we begin integrating our instincts with our emotions. It magnifies our intuition to a level that is unparalleled. We have a much deeper connection to ourselves and others, helping us to feel a part of something bigger. We transform ourselves into a powerful intentional force for growth and true transformation.

While this book is about trusting in the brilliance of others, we have to learn that we can be brilliant too. The greatest insights just happen to come when we are emotionally balanced and working with a highly functioning intentional filter with the help of those who have already made the journey.

The better you can get at asking yourself about self-created errors and alternative explanations or viewpoints, the easier it is to break free of a damaging cycle of behavior. Then you can start accepting the brilliance of others and become the unstoppable person you were meant to be.

CHAPTER 6

Trusting in the Brilliance of Others

Imagine for a moment that that you were never trapped in your feedback loop. You could always listen to and take advice from people who have reached goals like yours. You always followed the direction of experts. How would that change your life? Wouldn't you *finally* break free of your old patterns?

Even when we have the confidence to start trusting ourselves and recognize when our protective filter sends us into spirals, we have to recognize that *real* growth comes from acting on the brilliance of others. None of us can do it alone—at least not without making a lot more mistakes, wasting precious time, and needlessly losing a lot of money. It's worth noting that the people with the highest spiritual and emotional development insist on checking with trusted advisors about the ideas and plans they've come up with.

No one is an expert on everything. In fact, we have reached a point in history where the average human is so specialized that they have a dozen areas of expertise. Even the specialties have niches. There are mechanics that are authorities on fixing cars, but some only work on hybrids. There are CPAs that only work with new businesses or only work with investors, for example. There are chefs for chain restaurants, and there are fine dining chefs and even personal chefs. Doctors have so many specializations it's ridiculous. But they all treat illnesses and prescribe medications. We work with all of these people, and many more, because they have a knowledge base and set of skills that we don't have. We recognize implicitly that each of these roles has practical and educational limits.

Suppose for a moment that you have a friend with several advanced degrees in nuclear physics. You might rightly consider him to be the smartest person you know. At the same time, you would be very hesitant to take his advice on fixing something he knows nothing about, such as clogged pipes in your bathroom, and you certainly wouldn't want him performing any major surgery.

When you consider things in that light, it's obvious you need to stop thinking of yourself as an expert in everything, because it just isn't true. We all need outside ideas and perspectives. It's also a good reminder that you have to be careful about the advice you take, since intelligence and intention aren't the only things that matter.

Who Can We Trust?

Of course, we don't want to trade our own bad advice for someone else's bad advice. So, how can we ever know who to trust? After all, we want to benefit from the brilliance of others. We don't want to get caught in the foolishness that just happens to flow from another person's mouth.

One of the best starting points is to seek the advice of other people who already have what you want or are well on their way to achieving it. If your goal is to make a million dollars, for instance, then you could look for mentors who have already climbed that particular hill. You *wouldn't* want guidance from someone living paycheck to paycheck.

There is no credibility like experience. If there is someone who can show us exactly how to get to where we want to go, we would benefit most from letting them guide us. Of course, we should check their qualifications before we start acting on their suggestions. It's unfortunate, but many people position themselves as "experts" when they don't really have the expertise or track record to back it up. Sometimes this happens for financial reasons. In other cases, it could be that the person just doesn't know any better. Some have big hearts and really want to help others, but they are just trying to "fake it till they make it." That might help their self-image, but it isn't going to grow anyone's bank account. You don't want to buy into ideas that just amount to another person's faulty plan.

Along the same lines, not everyone who has experience or perspective makes a great teacher. As an example, there are lots of people in the coaching profession who know a great deal about sales and marketing but aren't as well-versed in the art of change. They can definitely tell you what to do or how to do it, but they might not be so capable of helping you to get over the blocks or hurdles keeping you from the results you want.

In the personal development area, I have already pointed out the flaw in many mindset programs. The coaches teaching mindset are great people and believe wholeheartedly that the model works. They are actually right. It does work for high performers that are already using their balanced intentional filter.

For the vast majority of the population who are somewhere just outside of that high performer range, mindset programs will only work well after letting go the protective filter I've shared in this book. Until you are practicing the strategies in this book, mindset can cause more frustration than help.

You always want to be aware of someone else's motivation to help you or give you advice in the first place. It has been my experience that most successful individuals are eager to see others succeed. However, they may want you to prove that you're serious about taking the next step first.

There is a good reason for this: once a business professional makes it to a place in life where people can see that they're doing well, lots of pretenders tend to come out of the woodwork. They'll ask for advice and mentoring even though they don't really know how to follow through. This amounts to a huge waste of time for the professional so they will naturally become hesitant to invest their time and money in others who might not be willing to put in the work needed to succeed.

A few years ago, I connected with a successful stage hypnotist who happened to be doing shows in my area. I saw how amazing he was at his craft and wanted to learn from him. I asked him to train me, and he said no.

Over a series of nine months, I showed him how serious I was. Eventually he saw how serious I was and took me on the road with him for two months. He showed me everything he knew. It was an absolutely invaluable experience. I was able to learn firsthand about stage hypnosis, and I learned a valuable lesson about vetting people out as well as sticking to a plan of action when I want something. Before I had proven myself to him, I was just another potential time-waster who would turn my attention to something else in a few weeks.

Although some people will share their time and perspective because they happen to know you and want to pass along what they've learned, most of the expert professional, mentors and coaches have invested significant money in their education and want to be compensated in some way. This is where things can get tricky.

Great coaching and training are investments that pay for themselves again and again. Paying someone to teach you how to sell increases your ability to support yourself and your family. Paying for the knowledge of how to create the business you've always dreamed of reduces stress and creates fulfilment. Paying someone to help you clean your emotional filtration system makes the business, relationships, and life you have always wanted possible. It's a no-brainer. Learning the right steps forward can be an absolute bargain since they can not only lead you toward breakthroughs, but can also greatly shorten the amount of time it takes to reach your goals.

On the other hand, it is true: some people want to take your money without providing much of anything in return. They are not aware of their own protective filter advising them to take care of themselves first. They recognize that you might be desperate for answers, and they will tell you whatever you want to hear. You've undoubtedly run into these types of scams, and so have I. Unfortunately this group is also amazing at getting past other peoples' protective filter.

How do you tell the difference? The best answer is usually to just follow common sense. Think about the programs being offered and the promises being made. Are there fluffy pitches made around an emotional story? Are there vague, sweeping statements that seem to deflect your question? Do the methods sound logical to you? Do they listen to you and ask you questions about where you are at currently? Are there any verifiable results, pieces of research, or testimonials to back up what you are hearing? Does the person have training and focus that's relevant to what you need and want, or are they following some cookie-cutter system being developed and promoted by a third party?

Having the answers to any one of these questions doesn't necessarily lead you to a definitive conclusion. But when you put them all together, you will usually get a gut feeling one way or another. When in doubt, pay attention to the sales messaging and book a strategy session. Is the strategy session in line with the sales message? Do you feel like the coach has a good understanding of your situation and can help you? Does it feel like you're a good fit to work with each other?

If you want to break free of the pattern that keeps you stuck, you have to trust in the brilliance of others to get past your raw emotions and your protective filter. But getting bad advice is just another way of falling into the same trap. You want to make sure the insights you're getting are valid and you're not just following along because someone tells you exactly what you want to hear at any given moment.

How to Process Good Advice

Once you do find a person who has the system or answers you want, it's time to trust what you've heard and take action. You simply buy in. You go all in, without reservation, for a given amount of time to see how things go.

This can be a very difficult suggestion. After all, someone else's ideas can feel a lot like the thoughts you are used to obsessing over. It's only natural that your protective filter gets in the way. The protective filter will often engage in the beginning and cause you to overthink the advice. It will lead you to spend time and energy on questioning their strategy, and you might become hesitant to take action. Does what they say actually apply to your situation? You wonder if they *really* listened to your unique situation. You might even start believing that these experts are wrong and your way might be a better way after all.

None of that is going to help you, though, so it's important to break that cycle. Just decide to go "all in." Unless your life or the future of your business is on the line, you don't have a lot at risk. And sometimes, many times, that is the best reason to go all in.

I will address this more specifically in the next chapter, but everything is dependent on action. We can't change the course of our lives with great ideas or perfect thoughts. Eventually we have to *do something*.

We simply start listening to the advice and coaching we are given, act on it, and see how things turn out. We resist the urge to change the plan, to make it our own, or to put it off until another day. When we do our very best to follow the advice we receive, a couple of things are bound to happen.

When Christine and I hired our last coach, we simply followed the suggestions she gave us. We did not argue. We did not hesitate. We did not understand some of what was suggested, but we did execute. We did what we were told. We doubled our business in six months, and we continue to grow.

Our case is not special or amazing. In most cases with good coaching, you will begin to get the desired results. At the very least, you'll see signs that better results are on the way. That's only natural. When you trade faulty, self-defeating patterns for actions designed to lead you toward success, your business and your life will improve. To put it another way, when you stop digging your own holes, you cease to go further underground.

Alternatively, you may in some cases discover that nothing changes when you start following the new advice. You might even end up in a worse spot, feeling confused and frustrated. That's disappointing, but it won't happen very often. And even when it does, you still come out ahead because you now have a better idea of what will and won't work for you.

In these situations, using your balanced intentional filter, you learn something from your setbacks and are in a place where you're taking action instead of waiting for a perfect solution to come along. For example, while Christine was working for Starbucks, she encountered many different managers with varying styles and levels of emotional intelligence. In the various stores she went to improve, she noticed something interesting. She found that what she learned about what not to do and how not to lead from some of these managers who struggled was more advantageous than any productivity or leadership tips she picked up from the good managers. Basically we can learn lessons from any situation if we are working from our balanced intentional filter.

It is likely that you will go through the kind of process I've outlined and still at times get advice that isn't right for your situation. Unfortunately, it is much more likely that your protective filter is will alter or ignore good advice from someone who has been in your shoes and knows the way forward.

That's why you not only want to be careful about who you take guidance from, but also accept it without injecting your own ideas into the process (at least at first). You don't know what you don't know. You came to the people you asked for help from because you were at a sticking point. Great coaches are open to and ask for feedback because they understand growth—yours and theirs. Just do your best and keep the lines of communication open. And more than anything, follow their suggestions.

As you take action on their advice, you can compare your results to what you were achieving before and where you wanted to be. But until you take those first steps, you won't be able to figure out whether what you're hearing makes sense or not. It just becomes another thought, problem, or possibility in your mind. You must take action.

Far too often we tell ourselves that we're acting on the best advice out there when what we *really* did was skim a book or convince someone else to listen to us whine for a while. Then we went right back to doing the very thing we had planned on doing all along.

Other people know things you don't. They have the perspective to see things from the outside and provide an objective point of view. They have the expertise to navigate situations you did not know existed. To benefit from their brilliance requires admitting that you don't have all the answers and trusting they might be able to show you a better way forward.

Are You Afraid of Commitment?

At a certain point, every successful person learns that they can't advise themselves or be their own sounding board. When we try, we end up confusing ourselves and being even less consistent than we were in the past.

If you're serious about creating change in your life, if your serious about growing in your business, I would encourage you to think about engaging coaches that include an emotional mastery component in their coaching. If you think I'm making this suggestion for the wrong reasons, don't work with us. I want everyone to have the best opportunity for success

Get the best coach you can find. Make a budget to afford it. Look for someone with the strength to encourage you when you need it and to call out where your lie machine is activated. When you do, you'll discover they can help you zero in on truths and blind spots you didn't see before. I can tell you from experience on both sides that it's like having parts of your life illuminated before your very eyes.

You'll also learn something all good professional coaches know: you'll put more into the process when you've paid for it. One of the interesting things about human nature is we only tend to value things that cost us in a significant way. We've all heard free advice that ends up being worth what we paid for it. But when you've sought out a specialist and paid for their time, you get more from the process because it tends to be more focused *and* because you've put something on the line, you participate more fully. You don't want to waste your money, so you work harder on generating the change you want.

Commitment is the key. Remember that as we move through the last few chapters; be prepared to put these ideas into action.

CHAPTER 7

Committing to Action

I had a sales coach a few years back that said, "Nothing ever happens until someone sells something." What he was really saying is that nothing in this world ever happens, or changes, until we come to an agreement on something and take action. This is such an obvious fact that we often take it for granted. At the same time, it's so easy to get wrapped up in our own thoughts and emotions that we can trick ourselves into doing nothing for a *really* long time. We can get into the trap of thinking we have to figure out the details, get all the pieces in place, or perfect some part of our life or business before we move ahead.

For that reason, in this chapter I want to share a very simple suggestion that will aid you in getting more familiar with and seeing your protective filter. This suggestion of taking action will help you stop taking your own bad advice, and then *get you moving.* If you don't want to take that step, then there is really nothing else I can share to generate the positive momentum you are searching for.

If you feel a little twinge of concern at this point, know the sensation is normal. In reality, for those who are not used to it, there isn't a huge difference between picking up the phone to make a sales call (as an example) and jumping out of a plane. In either case, these events trigger our protective filter because we're trying to take on something that's massively uncomfortable. We're chasing a bigger goal. We can never jump halfway. It's all or nothing.

A vast many things that we were once scared of doing become fun and exciting later after we master them. As we become proficient or competent, we begin to like these things a lot more. It's always hard to take action, right up until the moment we've done something. Then we look back and feel like it was easy—or at least easier than our lie machine was making it out to be. That's why we either have to reach a point of desperation that forces us to take the next step, or simply decide to act intuitively based on the best information available to us. We simply have to take that leap of faith and trust in the brilliance of others. We have to trust that their accomplishments are something they can help us duplicate in our world if we want to see the growth we desire in our lives and businesses.

There was once a time when running a four-minute mile seemed impossible. Then Roger Bannister broke that barrier. It only took forty-six days for the next person to do it. Dozens followed after that. Sometimes, like Roger Bannister, we simply have to believe in what we haven't seen yet.

Out of Your Head and into the World

There is a magical barrier that exists between thought and reality. While thinking is an action, it doesn't produce anything except more thoughts, stories, and ideas. For example, we can wonder about what we should have for lunch. We consider all the varieties and possibilities until we find the right answer. If we spend too long, though, the time we set aside for our meal will be gone. It's only when we make a decision and act on it that something ends up in our stomach. The quicker the decision, the faster we get our result.

Action is the cure for the self-defeating cycle of inner thought. It's the one thing that makes it possible to stop the dreaded "what ifs?" and move on to "what's next?"

While Christine and I were in the Dominican Republic recently, we went on a fun water excursion. We hiked about an hour up a breathtaking wooded forest. On the way down we were to jump off thirteen cliffs or slide down natural water slides to into the river below. The water slides were very tame, while most of the cliffs were quite high. One of the people in our group began listening to her inner "what ifs." She ended up with analysis paralysis that comes with the overthinking I am talking about.

Christine and I took a different strategy because we both know how quickly our heads can convince us of a problem. As we all walked to the next cliff, we made the decision that the people guiding us were all jumping with such ease that we would simply follow them without thinking. We would just do what they did and think about it after we hit the water. We had the most amazing time, except for the time we spent waiting for the person who got stuck in her head.

When we start *doing things* instead of worrying about what might happen, our sense of doubt decreases. It has to because we're now engaged in whatever task or step is in front of us. We might still have reservations, but they'll float to the back of our mind as we focus on the given task. When we take action, we will have other, more worthwhile things to occupy our attention.

In the same way, actions you take in your life and business generate results. It's virtually impossible to change or improve anything in your life without different action—and sometimes it requires similar action with different people. Otherwise, you're just waiting for something to happen to you. As a rule of thumb, whatever happens to you without your input is often going to be something different than you wanted, expected, or hoped for. When you generate results from your intentional actions, though, you can evaluate them and make alterations going forward more quickly, thus bringing you success faster.

The obvious caveat here is that you don't want to take actions indiscriminately any more than you want to take advice without considering the source. For most of us, however, this is a very minor concern. We get ourselves into messes because we are used to following our own advice, hesitating too long, or simply refusing to take any action at all. We rarely get stuck because we've been doing things that made perfect sense in the first place.

So, if you've found a solution that's based on reason and experience, you can go ahead and take the next step. It can be a small one, if that's what it takes to break out of the spiral you are in. You can follow the recipe or roadmap that has been provided to you. You don't have to look back until you are far enough to know whether or not you're going in the right direction. Continuous monitoring is part of the growth process, but it should never prevent you from getting started.

Action Creates Momentum

When you start taking action, you'll start seeing the effects almost immediately. That's because the more you do, the more things will happen, and the easier it gets to keep doing more. It's much easier to course correct while you are in motion.

It's like pedaling a bicycle. As soon as you get on the bicycle, you are in a static position, holding the bike with one or both feet on the ground. You're not moving anywhere, and if you lift both feet up, it is tough to stay upright, unless you are an X-game trick rider. The first thrust of the pedal is the toughest, and it doesn't push you very far forward. After a few more pushes of the pedals, though, you notice that you are beginning to pick up speed. Not only that, but the resistance you felt with your first push is almost gone as you glide along effortlessly.

Get the bike moving fast enough and it will keep coasting for quite a while without any active effort on your part. You can speed up and change direction at will with minimal effort. In fact, it will take quite a while before eventually you come to a stop and fall over. Of course, on the other hand, ceasing to act for long enough will eventually cause you to slow down and fall over. If you want to move forward, isn't continuing to pedal a better choice?

That's also an accurate description of the way results work, particularly when it comes to measurable outcomes like sales, revenue, income, and even relationships. Every action we take is like pushing the pedal. This also applies to thinking. Thinking is like coasting without pedaling. It feels like we are moving but once we hit a harder incline, we go nowhere without pedaling. Without action, there is not one single thought that will benefit anyone.

When we begin working from our balanced intentional filter, our mindset shifts. We stop waiting for events to happen and begin intentionally directing the course of our lives and careers. At the same time, we're also affecting our intentional filter. We're now taking initiative and being proactive. These new results open us up to new opportunities and different possibilities, further altering and stretching our intentional filter in the process. Our imagination opens to the new possibilities. Our continued action produces definite results to alter our course while sharpening and honing our thinking, which leads to more activity, and so on.

What I'm describing here is a balanced intentional action feedback loop. More action leads to better results, which leads to an improved intentional emotional state, a stronger mindset, and further action. This yields even better results. This cycle is continuous and scales as we gain momentum. It is the same law of nature that Newton described. It is just now that we are using that law of nature for us from the beginning, instead of allowing it to work against us. It's the polar opposite of the situation I described in the opening pages of this book, where most people will see many obstacles and few opportunities.

It is taken as accepted fact that the rich get richer in virtually every part of the world. That statement is often used in a derogatory nature toward those who are rich. While it's certainly true that the rich often get richer, it's not only because of tax havens and other societal rules that keep wealth growing. It's mostly because the majority of successful people see opportunities and possibilities that others don't.

Wealthy people are often living in a more balanced intentional state. They trust in the brilliance of their accountants, financial advisors, and other trusted partners. Their protective filter isn't constantly feeding them bad news or telling them to give up. They aren't focused on all of the injustices they are experiencing. They aren't focused on protecting themselves from potential harm. They aren't focused only on getting the things that will make them happy. They aren't worrying about what strangers might think of them. They are focused on what is going to bring them the success they are looking for to engage in what truly matters to them. They are also looking for those they can help on their way to their success because they know that no one can do anything alone on the road to success.

Understanding the dynamic between emotion, action, and thought can be the insight that permanently changes your life. It's obvious to anyone like me who has studied psychology from most angles, and yet it runs contrary to everything people think they know about motivation and personal development.

Act Like You Mean It

There are millions, maybe billions, of people out there who would be healthier, wealthier, and happier if they would simply act like they wanted to be successful.

Think about how many people you know who would like to lose a few extra pounds. They spend countless hours encouraging themselves and looking for "secrets" that will lead them to a flatter belly. But the information they crave isn't lost, hidden, or hard to understand. It's simply tough to implement and stay committed. It takes a day-in, day-out discipline to achieve what they want.

Imagine if someone who wanted to lose weight stopped searching for all the motivational articles and instead looked up one single column from an Olympian or well-known trainer on getting in shape for beginners. Then, suppose they were to write down the plan that expert had provided and began following it step-by-step to the letter.

By skipping the usual process, they would miss out on that initial surge of inspired willpower. They might miss that pumped feeling we get from doing things like making New Year's resolutions. But guess what? They wouldn't need it because they would have already taken action. Then, when the next day came—that time when the first bit of willpower was running out—they would already have a clear idea of what to do next. They would have kept themselves going just by doing something instead of thinking about doing something. There wouldn't be any excuses about what they needed to do first because they had already begun. They would know that progress was possible because they would have already made some. As I said before, progress is easy when already in motion.

This example is simple and relatable. What's more poignant for our purposes is that the same principle applies to building a business and generating wealth. You can read all kinds of articles, attend dozens of seminars, and listen to all the things a top-notch mentor might say. But if you don't take action, none of that matters.

In fact, I would argue that getting yourself into a balanced intentional emotional state is more important than having a specific course of action. Because if you are not able to use your intentional filter, you cannot effectively use your action-oriented mindset. That's why the work Christine and I do pays off in such a big way for so many people. We stop people from overthinking. We teach them how to let go of their protective filter and use their intentional filter. We get them to start moving into a powerful growth mindset.

No one ever wakes up completely out of shape and feels like going for a run. There was never a salesperson or entrepreneur in the middle of a slump who felt like hunting for fresh clients. We have to take action to get what we want most, and these desires come from our intentional filter, not from our protective filter or lie machine. It's only after we get the ball rolling and things are going great that we're internally motivated to keep up the effort.

It's easy to make deals when you're on a hot streak. You look forward to hitting the gym when you're already trim and fit. But you'll never get to that point if you don't get started. Unfortunately waiting until you have the right inspiration or emotional state doesn't work because it's exactly backward. To change results requires taking some intentional action, even if it's the smallest action. The first action I always help people with is cleaning their filter by learning how to identify how they're dominated by their vulnerable raw emotions. This leads them to their balanced intentional state that is the catalyst for all forward motion.

Are You Ready to Take Action?

Christine and I chose our company name very carefully. Generator Coaching & Consulting originates from our mission to help our clients generate the business, relationships, and life they've have always desired.

Most people focus on the implied social and financial benefits of that statement. For me, though, the key word is *generate*. I firmly believe that it is up to each one of us to generate what we want in life. It's clear that some sort of forward movement and change are needed, otherwise we are settling for what is given to us. Things simply won't happen on their own, no matter how many books you read, lectures or seminars you attend, or gurus you listen to. Nothing happens unless you take action, and you have to take the steps yourself. Only you can generate your success.

Somewhere along the line, we as a society got so wrapped up in the power of positive thinking that we forgot that we are emotional beings. Manifestation has become a huge area of focus. *The Secret* has misled many people into thinking they can just think what they want into existence. We have fooled ourselves into believing that thinking is the generator of our lives. That is not the way it works. While stuck in our protective filter, our thinking is the generator of mayhem.

The reality is that it is our unconscious, emotional world that is the key to get things done. All of our aspirations, motivation, and inspiration come from our balanced intentional filter. From there our thinking is on a new plain of existence. Our mindset is aligned with our intention. All of our goals and attitudes are connected deeply to our purpose, and when we address our emotions, we grow exponentially.

If you truly want to change your situation, you will want to bypass the protective filter of your own doubts and ideas. You will want to commit to trusting others and yourself. You will want to take that leap of faith. Only then can you experience the growth you desire.

Are you ready? Take a moment to really think about your answer, because the next steps in your business or the life you desire depend on that answer. If you feel like you're truly prepared to start generating your course—and you are willing to stick with it long enough to get real results—let's discuss how to bring all of these ideas together.

CHAPTER 8

Making a Decision

Nearly twenty-five years ago, I had to make a choice: Did I want to stay on course for a long, miserable, unfulfilling, bitter life, or did I want to try branching off in a new direction? It wasn't an easy call. I was frightened. I ran my life into a wall. I didn't know how to succeed with anything. I had a lot of talent, but my life was skewed by my protective filter. I had no idea where my journey would lead at the time. I knew I couldn't bear to live with the disappointment I felt every day. The fear of the unknown at that time was devastating. However, I took the leap and started following the advice of some very great people. My life changed amazingly and dramatically.

There is a saying that for every level there is a new devil. We all hit roadblocks, hurdles, and plateaus. We all have a choice. We can let that plateau be our final resting place or we can take that leap of faith and go all in.

Although your circumstances are probably way better than mine were, I want offer the same kind of choice. Do you want to stay stuck in whatever patterns are holding you back, frozen at whatever level of current success you've achieved so far, or are you willing to step into an unknown filled with great possibilities? Will you settle for what you have or reach for something greater?

I can't answer that for you, of course, but I am excited for you if you've stuck with me to this point. And I'm excited that you're ready to go just a little bit further. Once you do, everything else changes.

Anyone reading this book can ditch their protective filter and find a state of balanced intention that will lead to becoming a high performer. You simply have to be willing to shed old patterns of behavior to get it. Once you take intentional action, you get new results. Any adjustments that come after that are going to be in a growth direction. Nothing begins, though, until you make the decision and start the process.

Why Decisions Matter

In some ways, you could say actions and decisions are interchangeable. You certainly won't start doing something new until you actively decide to do things differently. Still, it's important to actually step out of your comfort zone and take action. Powerful things take place when you make decisions. A decision is a declaration. It combines action and commitment into a single sensation.

When I made a decision to become a psychologist, it was a declaration to the chef I was working for. I had no idea at the time that I was actually up for the task. He asked me what I wanted to do with my career. He was about to promote me to sous chef. I answered, "I think I want to become a psychologist." A short time after that, I started school. I made the decision that day, and it took ten years to see my decision to completion. It was the daily action that made this decision real.

I've already mentioned that when it comes to making decisions, people have a hard time. They have a tendency to overthink themselves into loops. They flip-flop on ideas. A thought comes, and they dwell on it. They start thinking about all of the dreaded "what ifs" associated with it. They start thinking of a new idea. Its human nature to avoid pain, and after our protective filter gets ahold of an idea, the decision gets even tougher.

To help my clients break out of this cycle, I have them make declarations. We write things down. You would think there wouldn't be a big difference between a thought that's in your head versus the same idea put down on paper, but an interesting thing happens when it gets transformed into print. It becomes real, and the protective filter cannot change it anymore.

Here is why: when the idea is in our head, it is at the mercy of the lie machine. Our emotions trigger a thought. Our mind reflects on it, spins it, and shapes it. As we continue to think on it, it morphs into something new, bigger, and scarier. With each thought, it compounds further into a bigger problem, a bigger monster. Once we've put it on paper, though, it is tangible. We can then evaluate the idea based on where it is at the present time. Coincidentally, this is one of the reasons people have trouble writing books and articles. They have lots of ideas, but they never commit them into a solid form because that makes them real.

Going back to this idea of putting things in print, though, imagine making a list of all the things you could do to get started on your next goal. You might think up dozens, or even hundreds of tasks. Then, imagine picking out the three most urgent and important ones. Now, narrow it down to that single one that would either have the biggest impact financially right now or make all the other ideas possible.

In the beginning of that assignment, you might feel overwhelmed, as many of the clients who work with me do at first—that's natural. But, by clarifying your reasons, the next steps, and the right order of priorities, you do away with all the extraneous possibilities. You end up with one actionable item. Then you simply do it. The next action is determined by the results of the first action. It's as easy as dominos. One action identifies the next. Step-by-step.

While the focus of this book is helping you reach your professional goals, we all have more goals than we are likely to pursue. When we let ideas roam free in our minds, they are like a swimming school of fish. From a distance they are numerous and fascinating and constantly changing direction. Once we grab one, pull it out of the water, and put it into a cooler, it becomes less slippery and easier to study.

By writing things down and examining them, we can decide which fish to keep and which ones to throw back for another day. The great thing is that our ideas are not fish—they don't die, and they don't go bad. By writing down every idea we have, we can act on them whenever the time is right. That's a clear and effective form of decision making that will always lead us to the next steps still to come in our journey.

Responsibility versus Accountability

Sometimes the decisions we make are going to be wrong. They will fail to work out because we made them based on incomplete information, or possibly because circumstances changed. In some cases, we might even decide that the goal we were focused on doesn't matter as much to us as we might've thought.

These might sound like failures or setbacks, but they are actually steps forward. Remember, movement doesn't just advance us forward; it also clarifies our vision. Even if we do the *wrong* thing, we'll end up with a better idea of what the right one looks like. Even those ideas of right and wrong can be subjective. It's up to us to write our own script and find our own success in our own way. A coach or a mentor can make the process faster and smoother, but in the end you still have to decide what matters to *you*. You will be the one living with the results.

That's not what most people are used to. Even entrepreneurs typically come from backgrounds where they've been given strict guidelines to follow from teachers, parents, or supervisors. If you're going to generate the business and life you love, you'll have to break free of those notions.

One thing that often surprises our new clients is that we don't focus on accountability. If you aren't familiar with the concept, this involves having a coach review your goals with you (as though you were a child) and schedule check-in calls periodically (maybe once a week or once a month) to see how you are doing with them.

We believe that if you need us to hold you accountable, you must not really want what you say you want. We focus on helping you connect to your internal motivation for what you really want so that you follow through on your plans because you want to. We don't want you to be dominated by the idea that someone is going to be looking over your shoulder.

Accountability sounds nice in theory, but it doesn't work for us. One reason is that we don't believe our clients need babysitters. Another is that it introduces micromanagement into the equation. We believe our clients come to us because they want to make changes. They want to grow their businesses. Micromanaging people for results is not coaching, despite what many people believe. It does not create ownership or a sense of personal responsibility. In fact, in those situations, the action tends to last as long as the accountability calls. Even more, it tends to harm the coaching relationship. That doesn't just make sense to us.

Even more important is the notion that action, or the lack thereof, will show you where your priorities lie. If you simply can't motivate yourself enough to make more sales, then it's probably a good sign you aren't really being driven by the goal you've identified. Having us badger you about it won't help. That's why we focus our energy on helping you identify unconscious biases and blocks. We believe in helping remove the protective filter that creates your mental blocks. We help you view your business and your life through your balanced intentional filter. This will indeed make you a peak performer.

A friend of mine once said that the only true bondage is absolute freedom. We coaches are only guides. The results of your actions are yours and yours alone. Each of us has a responsibility to ourselves and our loved ones to do our very best. We firmly believe that the consequences of each person's actions are meant to be theirs. We believe in responsibility.

Improving the quality of your business, relationships, and life is your responsibility. At the end of the day, you are the one who has to live with the results, for better or worse. We want you to make decisions and then be responsible for reaching your goals. We believe that your successes are ultimately up to you. We see ourselves as progression partners or partners for growth. We want to celebrate your successes with you, not force you to achieve them. If you aren't compelled to achieve them, then the issue is with your protective filter, the targets you set, and the way you see yourself, not our level of holding you to your word.

What Will Your Life Look Like in Five Years?

There is an easy way to tell if someone is emotionally balanced and successful or not. You simply ask them what their lives will look like in five years.

Someone who is focused on their goals instead of on self-doubt can paint a pretty detailed picture. They know where they're going and how they plan to get there. Conversely, a person who feels dominated by their emotionswill give a vague answer or admit that they have weak plans that might be changed by the smallest turbulence of life.

The big difference between these two groups is that one has made a declaration, a decision about their future, while the other hasn't. Those who are in balanced intention have committed to a plan of action and are likely to see it through.

This observation requires a couple of caveats. One is that commitment and decision making are different than traditional goal setting in the way that is so commonly taught now. I am *not* telling you to go home and create a vision board. That can be a fun activity, but if you truly believe in what you want, you don't need a vision board. As I know you understand by now, just thinking about things doesn't make them true. Being decisive involves identifying a first step and then taking that step so that your sense of belief can catch up later. Commitment generates belief.

The second caveat is that making decisions doesn't stop life from throwing curve balls. You are still going to be thrown back, pushed down, and otherwise derailed from time to time. If you are taking action from your balanced intentional filter, though, you can take these issues in stride without having them affect your vision or self-image.

As an example, I'm writing this book during the 2020 COVID -19 pandemic. There are lots of very real things happening in the world, and each of us is affected whether we believe in the virus and its consequences or not. Once again, we find that positive thinking (on its own) comes up short when the rubber hits the road. Repeating mantras all day and telling ourselves we will make it through doesn't magically heal the economy. It doesn't protect us from biological threats, and it doesn't solve boredom or financial issues.

However, that isn't to say that our lives are completely out of our control. Creative entrepreneurs are continually finding new, innovative ways to do business. People like me are taking advantage of the time to write books, develop courses, and increase their own knowledge. All of this is happening while we're continuing to grow our business. Those with an intentional emotional state are admitting and facing up to their doubt and fear. They are identifying their vulnerable raw emotions so they won't be dominated by the noise in the world, whether it's the news or social media. This allows them to see the world through their balanced intentional filter. This provides them with the solid resilient mindset to keep going without having to pivot or drastically change the way they do business.

In other words, when we have a clear vision of what our life will be like a few years from now, this crisis (or *any* crisis) won't stop us. Our plans might change, and we might take a slightly or completely different route than we had envisioned, but we won't find ourselves standing still or going out of business because we are paralyzed by fear.

One of my friends lives in California. He opened a food truck about eighteen months ago. I watched and even helped him put it together. He was just hitting his stride and making money when the pandemic hit. For a couple of weeks he was dominated by his raw emotions. His protective filter told him he was going to lose his business. We talked about his situation. We even joked about masking up and going neighborhood to neighborhood. Then, from a more balanced intentional filter, he actually put a plan together for safety and cleanliness and was back in business.

This once again illustrates the power of making a decision and sticking to it no matter what. It's easy to react and simply follow your whims and impulses or even just quit. It's harder to begin acting intentionally as you move forward. With that in mind, let me ask you once more: Are you ready to quit taking your own bad advice and take the action to generate the business and life you've always wanted right now? What different action will you take?

CHAPTER 9

Accelerating Your Growth

You could take everything I've shared in the previous chapters and put them to work today. You could stop relying on a faulty protective filter, learn to trust in your own brilliance and the brilliance of others, and begin getting the results you want in your life.

Unfortunately, you probably won't.

The truth is that you and I can achieve the success we deserve. It's just very difficult to reach it on our own. It's one thing to understand that we've all become accustomed to ineffective patterns of behavior and thinking. It's also important that we understand that behavior and emotion is taught wrong and has confused us for years.

Furthermore it's vital that we realize that's why our minds trick us into taking our own bad advice again and again. However, it's a very different thing to put the concepts to good use in a way that leads to real and lasting change and the success that follows.

It's almost impossible to notice our own blind spots, much less correct for them. That's the reason our protective filter keeps us in those patterns of thinking and doing the wrong things in the first place. If we aren't even aware of our own bad habits, the lie machine or faulty assumptions, how can we be expected to shift them?

The answer, of course, is to trust in the brilliance of others. Specifically, to engage with professionals, whether coaches, consultants, lawyers, financial advisers, or mentors who can guide us through the steps needed to follow through. If you're serious about making the journey from where you are today to the mental and financial peak you're aiming for, working with a coach is a great next step.

I am very direct about the fact I think you should hire a coach because I know the value of good coaching. I know what working with a variety of coaches has done for Christine and me. A good friend and partner of mine says everyone would benefit from have two mentors and three coaches. I couldn't agree more. Coaching shortened the distance between our circumstances and the life Christine and I wanted. We have seen the benefit in our business, and we personally don't plan to ever be without coaches. We are true believers.

Christine and I decided to write this book because we created a coaching business built upon the ideas in this book. We have proven that these foundational ideas are the most effective way to help people achieve their full potential. This book is meant to be a guide for those who are just beginning their search for insight, as well as those who have been on the journey for some time. It will also help those who are looking for a way to make their mindset training actually work. This book is a starting point.

In this final chapter, we want to give you a quick preview of the coaching process. We will explain why we think it's something that can help any willing entrepreneur, investor, or executive put our concepts to work.

How Coaches Help You Move Forward

A good coach brings two extremely valuable things to the table. They bring expertise based on experience, research, and education. They also bring an outside perspective. It's virtually impossible to get either of these on your own.

While earning my doctorate in psychology, I spent several years working with dangerous and aggressive inmates in correctional institutions and community mental health facilities. I built my own private practice until I realized that mental health was not a passion for me. For the last few years, I've worked with high performers, helping them step even higher. Christine brings a wealth of experience in leadership, productivity, and systems improvement. I am an expert in emotional mastery and emotional intelligence. Both Christine and I also focus on motivation, leadership training, communication, and the art of achievement.

There is an abundance of positive mindset coaches and gurus out there. However, very few of them are able to look at the mental/emotional side of performance issues with our kind of background. We want coaches who know more than what a certification program or a cookie-cutter course says about asking the right questions. The very best coaches have the ability make change happen fast. They have a talent for inspiration and can transfer their knowledge and inspiration in a clear, actionable way.

Even if you could teach yourself to think differently, be your own sounding board, or download some sort of hypnosis app for your health on your phone, it would only help until your emotions were triggered. Then you would fall right back into the pattern you were accustomed to. While a coach's background is important, it's also important that coaches don't live in their own mind so they are not as susceptible to our lie machine. They need to be able to bring our unconscious biases to our attention.

We've all heard and you probably understand very well by now that we can all be our own worst enemies. Trapped in our protective filter, we can easily fall back into our ineffective cycle of overthinking and inaction. We shoot ourselves in the foot again and again. Sometimes what we need more than anything else is for another person to step in from the outside and ask: "How is that serving you?"

A great coach can do that in a way that is illuminating, humorous, constructive, and unbiased. It's not difficult to find opinions about what you should do, or where you might be getting things wrong. Too often, though, we take advice from people who either don't know or won't share their opinion honestly. Friends and relatives don't want to hurt your feelings, colleagues think in terms of their own businesses and challenges, and employees don't have an incentive to speak up for fear of rocking the boat.

We all need guidance from someone who is trained, certainly, but also from a person who is not afraid to tell the truth. We all want to hear what's going to work as well as what's not going to work. I had a coach a few years back who always encouraged any idea, even though some of them were flawed and not well timed. After hiring another coach, I realized how detrimental was. The right action at the right time is imperative to grow and scale in an effective manner. We all need firm and fair honest feedback—not just feedback that feels good in the moment.

A lot of coaching programs are filled with BS. They include a few accountability calls, but many consist of the coaches just telling you that you have the answer inside you. This isn't really useful, especially when it comes to growing and scaling businesses. Talking about how great you're doing as you feel yourself spinning is not a real plan for growth. De-escalating the spin without clear next steps doesn't help either.

These situations happen because some coaches are out of their depth. Other coaches simply don't have any vested interest in you or don't know how to challenge you. This turns into pointless sessions of celebration and encouragement without strategy or direction.

That might be fun, but you could hire a cheerleader or a clown and get the same results for a lot less money. You need a coach that will celebrate your wins with you, but also give clear direction and call you out when you're being stubborn, resistant, or stuck taking your own bad advice.

What Is Coaching Like?

Every client and situation is different, so there isn't a set playbook for coaching to follow. There are definitely cookie-cutter programs out there, but they don't help the majority of people grow personally or professionally. Still, you might be wondering what it's actually like to work with me, Christine, or another professional. Maybe a fear of the unknown has even stopped you from working with a professional coach up to this point.

Naturally, the work you do with a coach will involve a number of questions. Great coaches are going to help you dig deep to find out where you're at, what you know, and which areas of your life or business are causing you pain at the moment. Gathering the facts to create a foundation can seem like an overwhelming process. It's really not hard unless you're overthinking the answers. Then it's a little tougher, and that's a sure indication that hiring a coach is a great move for you. It's worth it, though. Coaching brings certainty and a step-by-step strategy to your business and your life. We *always* help our clients learn things about themselves that they were previously unaware of.

People don't always know where the gaps in their business, relationships, and life are. You can't work on things you aren't aware of. You can't always see spirals that are taking place on an unconscious level. We might feel their effects, but as hard as we all try to identify what is causing the spiral, we all struggle to identify the causes sometimes.

This is because we all tend to look outside ourselves. You simply cannot look inside yourself without someone outside helping you.

We have worked with entrepreneurs who didn't understand the (obvious) reasons why their sales calls were failing. We've met men and women who couldn't ask for the sale. We've had a remarkable number of people who did not know how to talk about what results they offered to people. They were extremely well versed in how their product or service worked, but they could not tell us what that did for their customer. We've come across otherwise bright professionals who either dominated their colleagues or were crippled by self-doubt. We've seen business owners sabotage themselves by pouring money into huge marketing campaigns with no focus or at the wrong time for their business.

You might be thinking that you would never make these kinds of mistakes. You might be right. But ask yourself this: If you have all the answers, wouldn't you be getting different results?

Lots of things are easy to pick up when you have the right training and a healthy third-party perspective. And some of the biggest and most obvious problems that sink businesses and destroy dreams are utterly invisible to the people who need these answers the most.

If you learn nothing else from this book, understand that you aren't going to think your way out of your own problems. Reading, attending seminars, and checking out courses can help. But if you're really serious about getting different results faster—if you want to stop talking about what you're going to do and actually get it done—it all starts with your emotions. Mindset is only half of the equation. You need a strategy to rid yourself of your protective filter so you can start working from your balanced intentional filter. The best decision anyone can make is the decision to do it with a coach qualified to help you do that.

Are You Ready to Jump on the Bullet Train?

When people ask us what we do, we rarely ever walk them through specific steps or processes. We simply and succinctly let them know that we help high-performance business professionals who are struggling with hitting their next income goal make their next six figures in record time. Instead of going into boring processes, we paint an exciting picture that's easy for any entrepreneur or business person to understand.

Imagine for a moment the life you want to live. Visualize your normal average day in your mind. Picture the relationships you want to have, the house you want to live in, the amount money you want to have, the car you want to drive, the people you want to help, and the kind of activities you want to do during your day to be successful. Now envision the path that leads from your current circumstances to that destination.

Is that picture a little fuzzy to you? Do you sense that there is just too much ground to cover? Do you find yourself discouraged because you've tried to make it so many times before? Is it so out of reach that nothing came to mind outside of what you already have?

Now, imagine that you have a guide—someone who could step in and help you clear away all the head trash, distractions, and excuses that sits on the track between you and your goal. Imagine that they provide you with a ticket on the bullet train with two stops—one at the start and one at the end. Wouldn't you want to follow that guide? Wouldn't you want to get on that train? Would you insist on trying to hike the distance on your own if the tracks were right in front of you?

That's what great coaching is like. A great coach brings you clarity you simply don't find on your own. We've seen it again and again. Early in the coaching process, awareness and understanding shift. That's when clients get off the emotional roller coaster of frustration, procrastination, and overthinking and start speeding toward their goals. Everything begins to move more quickly than it ever has, simply because they are not reinventing the wheel; they are not overthinking its construction or debating whether it will actually roll the way they want. They are now implementing what the expert suggests. Whether business or person development, they are free to speed toward whatever it is they've always wanted.

After applying the process that we shared with you in chapter three about quieting the noise, you will begin to take in information in a new way. You aren't being weighed down with emotions and patterns that aren't useful to you. You are much more able to accept whatever the day week or month brings and respond in a proactive way.

Those who have applied these principles and did the exercises suggested in this book all have one thing in common. They knew they wanted more and were willing to do the work required to get it. They did the work to align their conscious mind with their unconscious emotional world. They learned how they were getting in their own way. They learned to communicate in an emotional way that deepened their relationships with themselves and then with the rest of the world. And they learned how to live intentionally. They became the high performers they always desired to be.

Still not sure you can do it or if coaching is even for you? We get it. You don't have to be sure about it. If you simply want to have a conversation about what it would be like to take the next step in your journey, or accelerate your path, contact us today over the phone. Mention that you've read this book, and we'll schedule you for a complimentary strategy call. That will give you a chance to see what it's like to chat with us and work with our team. Then we can each decide whether it makes sense to move forward.

Our mission at Generator Coaching & Consulting is to put our clients in motion and help them create results. If you're tired of trying things that don't work and want to turn emotions, thoughts, and actions into a balanced intentional plan for ultimate growth, then we want to hear from you.

Remember, it's up to each of us to decide to generate the business, relationships, and life we've always desired. We look forward to helping you achieve your vision, your goals, and your dreams!

READY FOR THE BULLET TRAIN?

Job stress costs US industry over 300 billion in annually in health costs, absenteeism, and poor work performance. We know that Emotional Mastery is the solution. If all of your overthinking has you stuck, hurting your performance or causing you to hate what you do, this is the time to master your emotions. Our simple Emotional Mastery Process is easy to implement with Dr. Terry Wager's concrete coaching and training. This is where transformation happens so you can truly generate the business, relationships and life you desire. www.emotionalmastery.com

NOTES

NOTES

NOTES

Made in the USA
Coppell, TX
05 February 2021